THE LOVE OF CHRIST

CALVIN B. ROCK, PH.D.

Pacific Press Publishing Association
Boise, Idaho
Oshawa, Ontario, Canada

Edited by Glen Robinson
Designed by Tim Larson
Cover illustrations by John Steel
Typeset in 10/12 Century Schoolbook

The author assumes full responsibility for the accuracy of all facts and quotations cited in this book.

Library of Congress Cataloging-in-Publication Data

Rock, Calvin B.
  The love of Christ / Calvin B. Rock.
    p. cm.
  ISBN 0-8163-0962-0
  1. Bible. N.T. Thessalonians—Criticism, interpretation, etc.
I. Title.
BS2725.2.R635 1991   90-22685
227'.8106—dc20   CIP

91 92 93 94 95 • 5 4 3 2 1

Contents

Introduction

Paul introduces both of the Thessalonian letters with reference to the "work of faith" (1 Thessalonians 1:3; 2 Thessalonians 1:11). In doing so, he provides a reasoned response to the fanaticism that assailed the young congregation at Thessalonica, as well as the extremism that often afflicts us today.

There is no question regarding the primacy of faith in Paul's theology. It is that armament which he lists "above all" (Ephesians 6:16). It is a practical faith—a working relationship, a dynamic principle of change and inspiration—that possesses the believer.

Paul sees this faith working *in* the believers (as in 1 Thessalonians 4:1-12), producing the fruits of righteousness. He sees faith working *through* the believers (as in 1 Thessalonians 1:8 and 2 Thessalonians 1:3), performing good works for others. And he sees faith working *for* the believers (as in 2 Thessalonians 1:4, 5), that is, laying claim to the merits of Christ whereby the developing believer is counted as "acceptable to God." This latter work is the paradoxical faith that saves by doing nothing—nothing, that is, but relying ultimately upon the grace and merits of Jesus. This is the quality of faith manifested by Abraham (see Romans 4:20, 21), who trusted in God's performance and not his own for the fulfillment of his needs.

An accurate view of Paul's faith, thought, and relations is absolutely essential for the church today, which, like the Thessalonians, continues to acknowledge its "undoneness" and to count its growing list of the dead while trumpeting the second coming of Christ.

Each of us is a recipient of the Macedonian call. Each is required by the terms of discipleship to cast body and soul into the furrow of service, to be willing to be all or nothing for Jesus. No better example of one's responding to this principle exists than the apostle Paul.

Chapter 1

The Love of Christ Constraineth Us

"For the love of Christ constraineth us; because we thus judge, that if one died for all, then were all dead" (1 Corinthians 5:14).

In 2 Corinthians 5:14 we are privileged to have one of the truly decisive utterances of New Testament writings. Here, after musing through several verses about the issues of life, candidly acknowledging his advancing age, solemnly examining the probability of death, and earnestly searching for the seminal motivation of his sacrificial devotion, Paul bursts through his mood of introspection to proclaim: "For the love of Christ constraineth us."

He has, of course, reasoned like this elsewhere. In Philippians 3:13, 14 he confesses to following after Christ but not having yet attained; in Romans 8:18 he concludes that present sufferings are well worth the joys of future glory; and in 2 Timothy 4:7, 8 he judges his life to have been a good fight and his reward a crown of righteousness. At these and other times, we receive glimpses of Paul's personal assessment of his faith struggle. Each statement is enlightening, but in no place does he link his spiritual effort with the grounds for his motivation more potently than in our text. Here, he encapsulates all that fires his energies, all that drives his priorities, all that thrills his soul, as the love of Jesus Christ.

What impresses us immediately is that Paul attributes his energies to Christ's love. It is not the power of Christ or the wisdom of Christ or the "otherness"—the transcendence of Christ—to which he owes his energies; it is His matchless love. Paul did not always know the love of Christ. In fact, until his Damascus experience, he was an enemy of Christ, "breathing out threatenings and slaughter against the disciples of the Lord" (see Acts 9:1). But while his physical eyes were for three days blinded at the home of Judas and with Ananias on the street called Straight (Acts 9:8-16), his spiritual eyes were opened to the redemptive works of Christ. Paul's days of blindness permitted God quality time to instruct and prepare him for service.

During those days of isolation, God's wondrous gift of His Son was indelibly seared upon his mind. Paul, who did not see Jesus when He was on earth, now saw Him "as of one born out of due time" (1 Corinthians 15:8). So memorable was his revelation, so real his view of the Saviour's life, that he was permanently affected, forever changed. Paul does not detail that which the Spirit burned upon his heart, but his witness thereafter makes it clear that he was shown the most poignant scenes of the Saviour's life: His mysterious condescension, His victorious living, His sorrowful passion, His painful death, and His glorious resurrection. How else could he write:

I delivered unto you first of all that which I also received, how that Christ died for our sins according to the scriptures; and that he was buried, and that he rose again the third day according to the Scriptures (1 Corinthians 15:3, 4).

And again:

Without controversy great is the mystery of godliness: God was manifest in the flesh, justified in the Spirit, seen of angels, preached unto the Gentiles, believed on in the world, received up into glory (1 Timothy 3:16).

Paul saw the cross, and he never recovered. For him, it was unspeakable, unthinkable, unimaginable, that the King would die for His servants, that the Judge would hang for the guilty, that the Creator would suffer for the creature, that the righteous Father would give all to redeem the profligate son. Paul saw it: the King of the universe leaving His throne to be born in a manger, to dwell among sinners, to be abused by humans, to die for the guilty, and to rise again as the eternal Representative of the human race. He saw it and was stunned, amazed, and he was ever grateful, ever awed—not able to comprehend its fullness but forever enamored by the fact that "the love of Christ constraineth us."

The Greek word *sunecho,* which King James's authors translated as "constraineth," is given a wide variety of meanings by students of the original manuscripts. The Modern Language Bible reads, "For the love of Christ *lays hold* of us." This means the love of God "arrests" us, it captures us. In this view, the apostle credits Christ's love as the clinching argument, the pivotal reason, the key factor in his conversion from enemy to friend. He had been Saul, the proud and selfish Pharisee. But when he discovered that "God commendeth his love toward us, in that, while we were yet sinners, Christ died for us," his heart was broken, his understandings were changed, his associations were changed, his priorities were changed, his habits were changed, his language was changed, his name was changed. He was captured, captivated, incarcerated, by the love of God, rescued from the kingdom of darkness and translated into the kingdom of light.

So thorough was his surrender, so final was his dedication to the love that now gripped him, that he could write: I am become a prisoner (see Ephesians 4:1), I am become a servant (see Romans 1:1), I am become a fool in glorying (see 2 Corinthians 12:11), "For to me to live is Christ, and to die is gain" (Philippians 1:21), and "I consider everything a loss compared to the surpassing greatness of knowing Christ Jesus my Lord"

(Philippians 3:8, NIV). Paul's greatest appreciation of that love was that it superseded all knowledge (see Ephesians 3:19), and his most earnest assessment was that it was more binding than death itself (see Romans 8:35).

Perhaps the cause of our lethargy, the reason for our apostasy, the root of our laxness is that our decisions too often have been driven by elements other than the arresting love of Christ. In the final analysis, no other reason is sufficient. Attraction to concepts or to organization, or loyalty to parents, or to church responsibility—none of these can arrest or overcome sin. It is the love of Christ, driven home by the Holy Spirit, that breaks up the fallow ground of our hearts, that melts the icy hardness of our souls, and that makes possible the quickening influences of the Word of God whereby we are born again (see 1 Peter 1:23).

The Revised Standard Version translates our text another way. It reads: "For the love of God *controls* us." That rendering differs, but is quite complementary to what the Modern Language Bible states. For, you see, not only must we be quickened, that is, brought to Christ and to the church. We must also be controlled after we come to Him.

Why do we need controlling? Romans 6:11, 12 helps us to understand. "Likewise reckon ye also yourselves to be dead indeed unto sin, but alive unto God through Jesus Christ our Lord. Let not sin therefore reign in your mortal body, that ye should obey it in the lust thereof." When we come to Christ, something marvelous occurs. The old man, the carnal nature with which we are born, is subdued. Having been quickened by the love of Jesus, our spiritual selves now dominate, Christ is enthroned within, and the old man, no longer fed the ingredients of sin, becomes famished, emaciated, immobilized, impotent.

The word *reckon* means to proceed as if the thing is true. It means that we should function as if the old man is gone, as if he has left us entirely. In reality, as long as we live, he is with us; there is no holy flesh. The bodies in which we function are corrupt and will continue to suggest evil patterns as long as we live. The flesh is a dynamo of sin, a wellspring of corruption. The essential act of obedience is that we feed the new man—Jesus

Christ—and starve the old man—the flesh. Result? The old man, once dominant, becomes a vegetable. Denied the usual sinful fare, immobilized by the lack of vital foods, he no longer reigns in our mortal bodies. But this condition persists only as long as the love of God is daily ingested. Faithful study, prayer, meditation, and fasting reinforce the love of Christ within us. Seen in His Word, in nature, and in our daily experience, that love molds and fortifies our hearts and minds in His likeness.

Why do we need the love of Christ? We need Christ's love to control our pride; our desire to be number one; our petty, selfish strivings for supremacy. We need it to control our passions; to control our appetites; to control our ambitions; to control our imaginations, our jealousies, our fears, our desires for revenge. We need the love of Christ to control us at the dinner table when we are tempted to irregularity and to excess. We need it to control us at the bargaining table when we are tempted to take unfair advantage, to extract the last measure of profit to the hurt of another. We need it to control us in the boardroom when we cannot have our way and in the bedroom when the lower passions strive for unhealthy expression. We need it to control us in front of the mirror and behind the wheel, when we are criticized and when we are praised, when we are promoted and others are passed over and when we are passed over and others are promoted. We need it to control us when we're embarrassed and misunderstood, when we're given blame we do not deserve and when we are given credit we are not due. We need it when we are denied just compensation and when we are returned more change than we are due. We need it to control us when we are all alone and no one is looking, and we need it to control us in the crowd when everybody is doing it. The love of God that lays hold on and convicts us also restrains and "keeps us from falling."

The songwriter asked the proper question when he wrote:

Will your anchor hold in the storm of life,
When the clouds unfold their wings of strife?
When the strong tides lift, and the cables strain,
Will your anchor drift, or firm remain?

And so is his answer:

> We have an anchor that keeps the soul
> Steadfast and sure while the billows roll;
> Fastened to the Rock which cannot move,
> Grounded firm and deep in the Saviour's love.

There are times in the press of life when every other mooring proves inadequate, when the undertow of sin pulls with almost irresistible force toward the abyss of transgression, when mind and body crave the satisfaction of evil, and only the love of God can bring us through. If we seek holiness for any other reason than this, failure is certain. The love of Christ is the only power that can keep us from falling. It alone can protect us in every high and stormy gale. When all other comforts fail, when all other defenses fall, when all other hopes have fled, the love of Christ remains.

And yet another view of our verse must be considered. It is that given in the Amplified Bible, which states: "For the love of Christ *impels* us." First, the love of Christ lays hold on us; second, the love of Christ controls us; and now, "The love of Christ impels us." We are reminded by this latter translation that the love of Christ is an exciting, propelling, stimulating, force. True, it *convicts* and *restrains*, but is also *arouses* and *propels*. When the realization of God's love illuminates our consciences, when we recognize the changes Christ brings to our lives, we are unable to compress our joy, to restrain our witness. We are compelled to share the fortune with others. The excitement of redemption, the joy of overcoming, the happiness of discovery that God loves even sinners like you and me drives us—impels us—to witness.

Christians, who, like Paul, have been smitten by the love of Calvary; who know the joy of pardon, the happiness of release from the binding grip of sin; who have experienced the relief that the gospel brings from the debilitating guilt of disobedience; who have been pulled as burning "brands from the fire," cannot refrain from telling of this love. We tell it not as would those who have read of rescue of others on some distant, stormy sea but as would the rescued themselves, as would one given up for dead—reclaimed from destruction through the sacrificial concern of another. And that is the impetus that causes us to sing:

> I was sinking deep in sin,
> Far from the peaceful shore,
> Very deeply stained within,
> Sinking to rise no more;
> But the Master of the sea,
> Heard my despairing cry,
> From the waters lifted me,
> Now safe am I.
> Love lifted me! Love lifted me!
> When nothing else could help,
> Love lifted me.

Every gospel tract dispensed, every Bible study shared, every dollar given, every hour of labor donated to the cause of God is motivated and stamped by the vibrant love of Christ that impels.

Armies of Christians have gone to the cross, to the stake, to lions' dens and firing squads, breathing at their last: "The love of Christ constraineth us." Vast numbers of God's people have gone to foreign shores, braving the dangers of hostile cultures, wild elements, and the pain of separation from loved ones, saying: "The love of Christ contraineth us." Millions of unnamed saints—penniless, obscure, and unheralded—have died in hope, faithfully fulfilling their Christian vow. Unknown, unseen, and unheralded, they have sacrificed gladly, saying: "The love of Christ constraineth us." And the rich and famous have shared in this expression also. Josephs in every land where Christ has been preached have stepped out of their usual company to claim the body of Christ. They have shared freely of their fortunes in the expansion of the kingdom. Admirers of the humble Galilean, they built monuments to Him while alive and through their wills and legacies declared in death: "The love of Christ constraineth us." That love impels us to holiness, it impels us to faithfulness, it impels us to devotion, it impels us to sacrifice, it impels us to forgiveness, it impels us to obedience, and it impels us to witness. It is a never-failing, ever-widening ocean of grace, too great to be fully understood but too overwhelming to be less than first in our hearts.

I know of no better way to explain what happens when one is massively impacted by a joyful event than to relate my own reaction to the birth of our first daughter. Each of the three girls was, and is still, special. But the experience of seeing for the first time a living form, a healthy bundle of tender life that was not only ours but that was *us*—cloned and reproduced by the mysteries of nature—was a thrill beyond compare. None of life's experiences before or after has so thrilled my heart.

She came at 1:00 a.m. on Christmas Day, and it was nearly 2:00 a.m. when I left the Winter Park, Florida, hospital. Not a choice hour to "tell the news," but I couldn't restrain myself. Those church members whose phones I rang and on whose doors I knock still smile at the recollection of the young pastor so excited as to throw away the normal courtesies and disturb their sleep with the news of that Christmas baby—I couldn't help it! I was overjoyed, overwhelmed, overcome, and that happiness demanded expression. I was impelled to share with my family and friends in cities near and far the joy that was mine. Encounter with Christ is like that. He brings knowledge and joy and relief and freedom and new habits and happiness that require expression. When He touches and changes our lives, we cannot remain silent, content to contain the blessings alone. We are impelled to witness. Our joy is impossible to hide or hold; it radiates in our voices, it shows on our faces, it animates our witness.

It was this principle that stirred the woman at the well, that unleashed the tongue of the blind man, that propelled Mary from the tomb, that turned Paul from his former traces and made him the most productive witness the church has ever had.

And if we will also hold faithful our gaze on Calvary, if upon our consciences there will also be stamped the unspeakable love of Christ, we too will know the confidence, the excitement, and the effectiveness of those whose motto is, "The love of Christ constraineth us."

The persecution that Paul and company endured in their missionary labors is typical of that opposition experienced by Christ's ambassadors in every age. Those who survive the storms of trial are those who are prepared by fellowship with Christ before the times of testing. Paul's advice to "come before winter" illustrates how and why.

Chapter 2

Come Before Winter

"For Demas hath forsaken me, having loved this present world, and is departed unto Thessalonica; Crescens to Galatia, Titus unto Dalmatia. Only Luke is with me. Take Mark, and bring him with thee: for he is profitable to me for the ministry. . . . Do thy diligence to come before winter" (2 Timothy 4:10, 11, 21).

Winter in Asia Minor is the worst of seasons. Cold winds howl out of the north, bringing paralyzing blizzards of snow and freezing blankets of ice. Often cattle become frozen statues in their stalls. Even in the mildest of times it is not uncommon for men and beasts to be forced for weeks to cease ordinary activity and struggle for basic survival behind doors. But it is true not only of Bible lands. It is true of most of the world. Each winter in the United States brings news of death and destruction due to weather-induced accidents and epidemics. Winter we can do without!

Spring? That's a different story. Spring is when the sun thaws the earth and gentle zephyrs blow upon freshly blossomed flowers, when butterflies emerge from their ugly

15

cocoons and the happy voices of children are heard lilting upon the air. True, the snows that winter piles upon the highlands often melt into raging floods, inundating the valleys below—spring, too, has its problems, but, compared to winter, give me spring!

And I like summer. Summer is for beaches and travel, for shining colors and cheerful spirits. No matter that sticky heat often forces us to hurry from one air-conditioned haven to another. No matter that the August sun sometimes bursts our thermometers and saps our energies. Nature is alive in the summer—the birds are singing, the sky is blue, life can be lived to the fullest. I love summer.

But, of course, autumn is, in some respects, the choicest of them all. The floods of spring are past, the heat of summer has abated, and the scourge of winter is still ahead. True, by late September, signs of death and decay already begin creeping into the foliage of the trees. But for a few precious weeks while summer wanes and winter delays, nature provides a respite, and the balmy atmosphere of rosy, red mornings and long, lazy sunsets make for the best of relaxation, as well as outdoor freedom and fellowship.

But, alas; inevitably, inexorably, unalterably, comes winter—winter that denudes the trees and discolors the lawns; winter that freezes the streams and ices the highways; winter that chills the bones and numbs the flesh; winter whose bitter blight makes it a fertile time for auto mechanics—and morticians. No wonder the aged apostle, chained in his damp Roman cell, urgently requested of his young friend Timothy: "Make every effort to come to me soon." "Do hasten and try your best to come . . . before winter" (2 Timothy 4:9, 21, Amplified Bible).

Paul's plea for Timothy's presence "before winter" is a poignant reminder of our need to prepare in times of opportunity for the inevitable adversities that life will bring. We often typify life's journey in terms of nature. We speak of life as having its valleys and its peaks, its nights and its days, its sunshine and its rain, and so forth. And the analogy is true. Life does have its seasons—its times of growth and its days of decline; its periods of peace and its times of war. Life is not one long, happy joyride of sunshine and smiles.

We all experience *winters of sorrow* brought about by the loss of friends and loved ones or some other such tragedy. I was happily rolling along in my sophomore year at Oakwood College, young and strong. All nature was alive and bright, and all was right with the world when one day in early January, I was told that I had a long-distance phone call in the administration building. I raced over to the business office, where excitedly I took the phone, only to hear my mother's voice saying, "Calvin, Sister is dead." Suddenly it was winter. I was dazed, confused, disheartened, and I remember stumbling weakly back to the dorm—not really knowing where I was or what to do next. The sun had unexpectedly gone down in my soul, and the cruel reality of life crushed my spirits— plunging me into confusion and depression that I had not known before.

But that happens every day to us Christians—the car wrecks, the drownings, the accidents, the heart attacks, the strokes—all these and a multitude of other heavy burdens suddenly dropped upon our shoulders are perpetual threats. These are the albatrosses of life, which produce mourning and heartache. In the world of life's experiences, winter is a daily possibility. The sunshine of any moment can be suddenly eclipsed by a letter, a phone call, or a telegram. We never know when, in the midst of sunlit days and star-filled nights, the stormy clouds of calamity will suddenly obscure pleasure and stifle joy, interrupting our comfortable rhythm of life. It happens again and again to some of us, and it happens sometime or other to each of us. Even the good suffer in this life— "Into each life some rain must fall." The apostle's words remind us—"Prepare in prosperity for times of adversity; come before winter."

The winter of old age—if nature is kind—is another crisis we must undergo. No ships entered or left Rome, where Paul was incarcerated, during the winter. The apostle knew that Timothy had to arrive before winter, if at all. So it is with life. The winter of physical decline is certain to follow the autumn of middle age. When it comes, it is too late to launch our ships of ambition, too late to dream dreams, too late to follow rainbows.

And how stealthfully old age arrives. Whereas our calendars boldly announce each seasonal transition, the gears of nature sometimes shift so softly that atmospheric changes are not immediately observable. Often winter zigzags into spring, spring melts into summer, summer blends imperceptibly into fall, and by the time we get used to the colors of autumn, the early blight of winter is already felt.

Life is like that. We move quickly from infancy and childhood to youth, but not quickly enough for the child. Children are always anxious to run into the next bracket. They are never six; they are six and a half or seven and three-fourths, or nine years and eleven months and ten days. Later on, we try to slow the process with pills and diets and dyes and spare parts. But imperceptibly we are nudged along, dragged ever outward to sea by the irresistible tides of life. With each breath we are carried further from the comforts of infancy, and childhood through youth, adulthood, middle age, and, if we are blessed, old age and elderliness. Then, finally, as our parents before us, we are cast into the yawning, insatiate grave. True, we live longer than recent generations. But the psalmist has warned us that even if we see "fourscore years, yet is their strength labour and sorrow" (Psalm 90:10). To be old, or "chronologically gifted," is to be honored by God, but it is also to be afflicted at last with the disabilities of frozen limbs and failing organs. It is often the loneliness of desertion by family; of mental and emotional relapse; of helpless existence in homes for the aged, where, if we are fortunate, we are given kindness and care as we wait for death. Robert Frost was right—"No memory of glory starred atones for later disregard nor keeps the end from being hard."

It is said of the longest survivor of all that he lived 969 years—"and he died" (Genesis 5:27). That is often a welcome relief to those sick and tired souls, whose trembling hands no longer keep the house, whose darkened eyes no longer focus, whose desires have failed, and whose once-strong backs bend low toward the grave. And since there is no escape from the pain of final disability, and since there is no glory in the graves to which we go, it is urgent that we prepare now for the inevitability of our sunset season, that we "come before winter"!

Another of life's certain trials is the winter of persecution. And this is especially true for the Christian. Did not our brother Paul also testify, "All that will live godly in Christ Jesus shall suffer persecution"? (2 Timothy 3:12). And the reason is clear: Satan hates Christ, and since he cannot kill Him again, he takes out his wrath upon His people. Of this Christ warned when He said, "The kingdom of heaven suffereth violence" (Matthew 11:12). These words, spoken to John's disciples, presaged not only the Baptist's gory death but also the persecution that Christ's followers through all ages would experience. Here, as in other instances, Christ warned His hearers of His approaching passion and of the animosities they would experience. And they did—Stephen was stoned, Peter was crucified, Paul was beheaded, John was exiled. In the centuries that followed, long generations of believers suffered similarly. Even today, in many lands to be a Christian is to be hated, and to be a commandment-keeping Christian is to be especially disfavored.

However, the most bitter persecution that the church endures is not that which is inflicted from without but that which arises from within. "Envy, suspicion, faultfinding and evil surmising" are manifestations of pride that wreak more havoc upon our individual and corporate purposes than all the efforts of governments and apostate religions combined. The child of God—church leader or believing parishioner alike—is tested more by the thoughtlessness of other members than by the ire of nonbelievers. It is when we are fired upon by our own troops that we are hurt the most. But since smiting by fellow servants is also a phenomenon of the end (see Matthew 24:49), the child of God must anchor deeply in that love which calls even Judas "friend." That is possible to those alone who "come before winter."

Finally, we should note that at the time of our text the

apostle was undergoing his own final season of life. Second Timothy is his last letter, his dying testimony. Paul was in bonds, falsely accused and subsequently convicted of instigating the burning of Rome—chained in a dark, cold, loathsome Roman cell. There he was preparing his final defense, his plight made bitter not only by the painful conditions of his bondage but by the desertion of Demas and others on whom he depended, so that he lamented to Timothy, "No man stood by me." No longer the vigorous evangelist of his younger years, he needed the physical and psychological support he was now denied. His was a winter of bitterest pain. In fact, a few month later, Paul paid the supreme price for his loyalty when he was privately led away and beheaded. But as he knelt with his head on the chopping block, he saw—Ellen White states—not the gleaming sword of his executioner, nor the green grass that was soon to receive his blood. Rather, he looked up "through the calm blue heaven of that summer day to the throne of the Eternal" (*The Acts of the Apostles*, p. 512).

And what was the source of the apostle's endurance? What was the fount of his strength for this and the other winters of trial that he suffered? Where did he find the power to joyfully accept the imprisonments, the shipwrecks, the floggings, the hungers, the hatreds, and even the execution that he now faced? The parchments! The parchments? Yes, the scrolls of the prophets. That dependence is expressed in chapter 4:13 of his appeal to Timothy when he wrote, "The cloke that I left at Troas with Carpus, when thou comest, bring with thee, and the books, but especially the parchments."

The cloak was an article of physical comfort. The books were articles of learning from which the wisdom of prior ages spoke to his inquiring mind. But the parchments, the holy scrolls, were the most coveted of his possessions, the source of his spiritual joy. "Especially the parchments" means that more important to Paul than either his physical health or his academic prowess was his relationship with his Lord. And that is instructive, for the parchments contain divine principles, heavenly promises, righteous provisions—and all the other ingredients necessary for victory. The influence of the parchments not only convicts and converts, it fastens, grounds, and affirms us in the faith.

Our experience with sin has been a winter of heartache for God and humanity; it has caused us 6,000 years of misery and death. And it has cost God the sacrifice of His dear Son. The storms have not yet ended, but the victory that was won on Calvary will come to full fruition when He shall "create new heavens and a new earth: and the former shall not be remembered, nor come into mind" (Isaiah 65:17). Until then, we shall be fortified by trial and strengthened to endure by the life in His Word. That was Paul's experience, and it can be ours as well, if we too will root our faith in the God of the scrolls and carefully obey Paul's prison plea—"come before winter."

Paul's "shepherd heart" is shown in his relationships with the churches he established. Timothy, his understudy, learned well from his mentor. Their example of service and fellowship with the people whom they baptized and nurtured is worthy of close study and evaluation, not only by pastors but by parishioners as well.

Chapter 3

When Timotheus Comes

"Now if Timotheus come, see that he may be with you without fear: for he worketh the work of the Lord, as I also do. Let no man therefore despise him: but conduct him forth in peace, that he may come unto me: for I look for him with the brethren" (1 Corinthians 16:10, 11).

During A.D. 51 and 52, Paul spent approximately eighteen months of intense evangelism in metropolitan Corinth, capital of the Roman province of Achaia. In Paul's day, Corinth was a bustling cosmopolitan seaport where Greeks, Romans, Jews, and adventurers from the whole Mediterranean world mixed in trade and traffic, offering conditions evangelists usually find very attractive. Some six years after his efforts there, the apostle was visited at Ephesus by a delegation that included Stephanas, Fortunatus, and Achaicus, who desired his counsel regarding issues of marriage, virginity, eating meat offered to idols, and certain other controversies that troubled the Corinthian congregation.

No doubt the apostle was cheered by the presence of the brethren. However, the visit brought him face to face with a

22

very delicate task: that of clarifying the distinctions between Judaism and Christianity without encouraging fanaticism or a feeling of triumph in the Gentile majority or without wounding the pride of the Jewish minority. Throughout 1 Corinthians, Paul exercises his usual genius in dealing with these problems. However, a contribution often overlooked but as important as any other in his presentation of Timothy is his perspective regarding pastor/people relationships.

He begins by saying in the King James: "*If* Timotheus come." A number of more modern translations read, "*When* Timotheus come." And it matters which is the correct reading, for even though both *if* and *when* are conjunctions, *if* is subjunctive, indicating that Timothy may or may not come; *when,* on the other hand, is indicative, thereby removing all doubt. Timothy is on the way! Timothy did go to Corinth, and his arrival there with Paul's letter emphasizes every church's need for ministerial direction and encouragement. No group is as woeful as a church without a pastor. A family may lose its father and the mother assume responsibility; an army may lose its captain and another rise to leadership; a crew may lose its foreman and someone else seize the occasion, but sheep must have a shepherd—the flock does not fare well without a guide. The church may not see their pastor every day or every week, but every Corinth needs a Timothy. Dying men and women need words of encouragement. Judgment-bound humanity needs an advocate—someone to stand between the living and the dead, someone to refract, reflect, and disseminate the light of God's Word. Our churches, sometimes defiant, sometimes dying in binding traditions, sometimes self-opinionated, belligerent, and self-satisfied, need preachers. A church needs a minister to bury its dead, to counsel its youth, to marry its young, to baptize its converts, to supervise its planning, to pray for its sick, to bless its babies, to comfort its dying, to conduct its rituals, to lead its liturgy, and to faithfully interpret the Word of God.

And the church needs *pastors*—not public relations geniuses, not construction managers, not salespersons, not business executives, not philosophers, not news commentators, not professional students—but pastors. The minster may, in fact, have to do a little of all of the above, but is, first and essentially, watchman and undershepherd, dispenser of the Master's grace, ambassador of His Highness—the King of the universe.

The pastorate is heaven's earthly link in the marvelous transaction of salvation: human instruments of a divine process, mortal integers in an immortal equation, the finite tools of infinite instrumentality, necessary and needed by God and humans.

Books have been written on Paul's Christology, his soteriology, and his eschatology. His profound positions in these areas are a perpetual challenge to Christian thinkers. But his words to the Corinthians regarding their treatment of Timothy remind us of his profound ecclesiology, particularly his counsel regarding pastor/people relationships. Paul himself was like the priest of Chaucer's *Canterbury Tales*, "a kind and gentle knight." His heart was warm, his hands were willing, his feet were busy, his love was magnetic, and his life was exemplary. He was a preacher's preacher, a writer's writer, but as much as anything else, he was a pastor's pastor—establishing Christian beachheads all along the shores of Asia Minor and Europe, erecting memorials to God in Athens, in Corinth, in Pamphylia, in Pisidia, in Berea, in Ephesus, in Philippi, in Lystra, and in Iconium. And, having built this wide parish, he maintained his presence through letters and visits, continuing until his death as an inspirational spokesperson regarding the affairs of the church.

While there has been only one Paul, each era of Christian ministry has produced its quota of servants, who, like him, have sacrificially extended the kingdom of God on earth. The men and women who do so today serve with differing backgrounds, talents, and methodologies. But all have one thing in common, like the great apostle before them; they serve with an accurate model of ministry.

There are several fundamental models upon which pastors base their endeavors; however, not all of them accommodate the pastor/people relationship that Paul had in mind. One very common view that fails the test is the one which says, "Here I am; let me do all I can for you," or "I am the pastor; I'm here to help you. Please give me your list of needs, and I'll see what I can do." Such a posture may result in some good. The pastor, who, by his actions and attitudes, thinks this way is usually well meaning. How else could one be so sacrificial, so willing? I have known such pastors. They visit the sick faithfully, they advise in legal matters, they transport the elderly to various functions, they provide food for the poor, they lay bricks with the deacons, trim hedges and cut grass with the janitor. Upon request, they will take members to the market or hospital or laundromat. They preach hard, work hard, pray hard, and, in short, burn out their lives for the people. Their style cries to people, "Pile it on. Load me up; that's my job. Here I am; let me do all I can for you."

The church with such a leader usually finds many ways to use and abuse such untempered zeal. Of course, the pastor should do everything possible for the people! However, the pastor who functions with this maxim will soon find that the bondservant's role involves more pickups than can be managed, more packages than can be delivered, more appointments than can be met, more phone calls than can be answered, more problems than can be solved, and, typically, while the pastor is suffering under the strain, the flock is perfectly willing to "let George do it." The Bible calls the pastor a watchman, a workman, a shepherd. And pastors must be all that, but a "Here-I-am-let-me-do-all-I-can-for-you" pastor eventually discovers that the task is impossible. They would do well to remember Jethro's counsel to the eager but overworked Moses, "This thing is too heavy for thee; thou art not able to perform it thyself alone" (Exodus 18:18).

The second stylistic assumption that must be avoided is the one that says to the people, "Here I am; do all you can for me." While the first model is that of the bondservant, this kind is that of the ruler/priest. Such pastors key upon Paul's words: "They which preach the gospel should live of the gospel" (1 Corinthians 9:14). They see themselves not as servants but as supervisors; they relate to their members more as honored guests than watchful shepherds. Their favorite place is behind the desk, where they can spin ear-catching phrases and profile splendidly. They shine at teas and banquets and other such social functions. They are popular at picnics and are available for any sort of high-visibility assignment. Mind you, they are scarcely to be found at the nitty-gritty problems of hard work. Their hands are never dirty. They are usually at home when the phones ring, and are not expected to show up for work-bees or work—period! Their attitude is not so much one of involvement as of directorship. Contrary to the Son of man, they come not to minister, but to be ministered unto.

Every congregation should be kind to its pastor. Pity the minister whose church ignores the special days. Christmases, birthdays, anniversaries, and vacations are ideal times to wish the pastor well. A word of encouragement, a card, or even, if possible, a gift, is sometimes in order. Tangible expressions are an excellent way to say thanks to the pastor and family. They say, "We love you, parson; you are appreciated." They say, "Welcome to the family; ours is more than a formal arrangement, you're a part of us; we appreciate your services." The balanced pastor recognizes the voluntary kindness of the people as a vote of confidence and good wishes. Wisely received, such kindness will not muffle the pastor's word against sin nor show favoritism or patronage. Faithful stewards are not lulled into compliant lordship by the thoughtfulness of members. To the contrary, as their comfort level is increased, so is their boldness for Christ and their effectiveness in service.

The real tragedy of the "Here-I-am-do-all-you-can-for-me" mentality is not that kindness leads to capitulation—it is that selfishness always seeks advantage of the goodness of others. "Here I am; do all you can for me" solicits favors as an expression of pride, and is an evidence of misdirected values. For such gifts do "blind the eyes." Not only are the people denied genuine expressions of love, but, like the house built upon the sand, this pastor/people relationship is doomed for failure.

"Here I am; let me do all I can for you" and "Here I am; do all you can for me" are both positions that may be occupied by otherwise nice people. However, both fall short of being accurate guides for pastor/people relationships. The first fails because it assumes a misguided understanding of the term *servant*; the second because it eliminates servanthood altogether. I suggest that what is required in proper pastor/people relationships is a third posture, one modeled by St. Paul. Not, "Here I am; let me do all I can for you," or, "Here I am; do all you can for me," but rather, "Here is Christ; let us together see what we can do for Him." This perspective is not one of a bondservant buried beneath the load of parish problems. Neither is it the self-servant living for the accolades of the people. Rather, in the truest sense, it is one of ambassadorship.

Such a posture develops at least two essential working principles. One is that of *invitation*—"Behold the Man." It points the people to Christ. It reminds them that He is the True Leader, the Chief Cornerstone of the church, the Rock of our salvation, the Bishop of our souls. It tells us that it is not "what" but "in whom" we believe that matters. This was Paul's enduring example. It is in this vein that he speaks of himself as "Paul, an apostle, (not of men, neither by man, but by Jesus Christ, and God the Father, who raised him from the dead)" (Galatians 1:1); "Paul, a servant of Jesus Christ, called to be an apostle, separated unto the gospel of God" (Romans 1:1); and "Paul, called to be an apostle of Jesus Christ through the will of God" (1 Corinthians 1:1).

Ambassadors are always aware that they are not sent to promote their own concerns, but those of their leader. Their credibility is not personal; it is provided by their exalted office. They are honored and respected because their leader is, and they bear special credentials, special powers, special authority in his name. The ambassador/pastor is boldly assertive—not exalting himself but his Lord—and the people can confidently respond because they know it is not the visible agent, but the word of their royal Leader that they hear.

The other working premise is *cooperation*. Stating, "Here is Christ; let us together see what we can do for Him" eliminates all imbalance of efforts. It demands of pastor and people equal dedication to the essential cause. And what sweeter relationship is there than that of a parson gently, but firmly, moving among the people, pricking their consciences and firing their zeal with the Holy Word, enlarging their faith with a holy life, corralling their talents with holy plans, and establishing their confidence always in the holy name of Christ?

Before leaving our text, we should note that while focusing on the pastor/people dialogue, Paul does something else instructive for healthy working relations: he demonstrates a wholesome generosity toward his protégé, Timothy. He doesn't treat him as a rival with potential to lessen his popularity among the Corinthians. Rather, he regards him as a fellow worker, a member of the same team, as part of a cause bigger than them both. Paul's words are: "For he worketh the work of the Lord, as I also do." Phillips, revised edition, has it: "He is as genuine a worker for the Lord as I am." Weymouth states: "For he is engaged in the Master's work just as I am." Goodspeed translates: "For he is devoted to the Lord's work just as I am."

Now, it could have been different. He could have said, "Now, Timothy is a good boy, but he's young and quite inexperienced, so please be nice to him." Or he could have said, "I wish I could personally be with you, but I am doing the next best thing: I'll sent you my substitute, Timothy." He could have "doomed him with faint praise" or slight innuendo. But not Paul. The apostle of service and sacrifice was too big, too secure, too anxious for the welfare of the church to allow pride or jealousy to tarnish his presentation of Timothy as one having common focus and authority.

His magnanimity was not false humility. It was not an affected or pretentious claim to selflessness; he was not proud of his humility. Paul had drunk too deeply of the cup of suffering for that. His own experience and his in-depth view of the sacrifice of Christ had cured him of the pompousness that once characterized his Sanhedrin labors. By his own admission, he was chief of sinners, not having fully attained. Whatever his thorns of the flesh, ungodly pride was not one of them. The greedy and proud can grow good gardens and manufacture great instruments; thieves and addicts can rivet together parts and make good automobiles; liars and drunkards can stick together long bridges and nail together handsome buildings; but it takes more than human genius to restore the quarreling parts of humanity. It takes the Holy Spirit. And as demonstrated at Pentecost, it is when leaders and people band in unity that this possibility becomes a reality.

We modern-day believers swim against the tide of human nature and human history when we crucify self and dare to follow the service principle of love. However, that is precisely what is required by God. Pressed together at the foot of the cross, we are washed in His blood, robed in His likeness, and equipped for His service. In that light, every human need becomes a Corinth opportunity and every sister and brother a Timothy with whom we can join hands for happy and effective ministry.

The essence of Christ's ministry is the reversal of humanity's fall into oblivion and their reconciliation with God. Knowing and identifying Christ as the Dynamo or the "Yea" of this process is the answer to the human dilemma and is vital knowledge.

Chapter 4

In Him Is the Yea

"But as God is true, our word toward you was not yea and nay. For the Son of God, Jesus Christ, who was preached among you by us, even by me and Silvanus and Timotheus, was not yea and nay, but in him was yea" (2 Corinthians 1:18, 19).

Titus does not bring good news. The Corinthian believers are upset with Brother Paul. Why? On two occasions he had promised to visit them, and both times he had failed to appear. The members took these delays as a sign of indifference toward their needs and sent word by Titus charging the apostle with unreliability, of saying, "Yea, yea," when he really meant, "Nay, nay." Paul's considered response is that due to travel conditions and certain tensions among the members, he had decided to write instead of attempting a personal appearance.

The intriguing part of this exchange, however, is neither the Corinthians' charge nor the apostle's defense. It is rather the way in which the evangelist uses the occasion to glorify Christ. He does so by expanding the principle of promise keeping raised by the Corinthians. Specifically, he contrasts the

promises made by converted individuals with those of the un-
converted. He then states in calm assurance that in Christ
there are no broken promises, no ambiguous declarations, no
duplicity or double talk—no saying Yes and No at the same
time, no saying Yes and meaning No, no fuzziness of meaning
or question of intent. Christ, he states, is God's clear, unsullied, uncompromising Yes. He is God's positive affirmation to
all the needs and questions and life. He is not Yea and Nay. In
fact, He is not Nay at all. Jesus is the One Sure Positive in the
confusion of life. In Him is the Yea!

And make no mistake about it. Life is a Yea-Yea and Nay-
Nay proposition. Our stay in time can be appropriately viewed
as a personal reply to the cosmic interrogatory, "To be or not
to be?" Each of us must examine life's options and decide
concerning its worth. And there are only two ways to relate to
the reality of our being—one is Yea and the other is Nay.
There are no neutral zones, no in-betweens. Every person's
life attests to one or the other of these polarities. We must say
Yea or Nay to this existence that has been forced upon us.

Those who say Yea are those who see life in a positive
sense, who live with courage and purpose. In spite of all of the
disappointments that come their way—all the tragedies, all
the treacheries, and the constant crumbling of their fondest
dreams—they maintain faith in the basic good of the universe.
They awaken in the morning with a zest for living and the
desire for personal success, as well as the good of others. They
spend their days expecting the best, interpreting even bad
events as steppingstones to a better tomorrow. They know
that "all things work together for good to them that love the
Lord." They are not oblivious to the grim realities of human
experience. They feel the pain, they see the dangers, they
understand the uncertainty of life. But having looked the issues squarely in the face, they have determined to address
them courageously. Their reply to the question of being is a
firm, unequivocal, faith-filled Yes!

There are also those who say Nay to life, and the naysayers
come in many shapes and sizes. They are first of all the cynical, those who see life as no more than a biological accident.

For them, humanity is simply the highest form of living things—creatures condemned to march the brief span of existence amid the vagaries of what Niebuhr calls the "step-motherly" whims of nature. Or, better still, they take company with Shakespeare, who typified life as but a tale told by an idiot, a comic tragedy without purpose or plan.

A second group of Nay respondents are the embittered. They have been crushed by adverse circumstances, soured by misfortune, and they see life as unfair and themselves the victims of a fate that is kinder to others. They are always stuck with the "old maid," or wind up with "the bear," and they never have enough "trumps." For them, the glass is never half-full; it's always half-empty. Thus, like the man who hid his talents and despaired of progress, they give up on life, ruefully fulfilling their unhappy days.

A third class who say Nay to life are the acquisitive. Their chief end is the acquisition of personal satisfactions, taking life as one grand opportunity to fulfill their material and sensual appetites. They are not cynical or bitter. They may even smile as they go about living, but they are selfish, shortsighted, greedy, and grasping. They have bumper stickers that read, "If it feels good, do it." Their creed is, "Do unto others *before* they do unto you," and, "Get all you can and can all you get." They sometimes earn law degrees and Ph.D.'s and retire in splendid respectability to the suburbs. But no matter what their status or how sophisticated their lifestyle, individuals who live for personal gain and comfort are negative to life. By their attitudes, they proclaim Nay to the foundation principles of existence.

And one more class of naysayers deserves mention—the frivolous or unconcerned. They go gallivanting through their years without giving serious thought or reflection as to who they are, why they are, or where they are going. It is not that they are cynical or bitter or acquisitive. They are, in a word, aimless, without goals, living for the moment only. Known as the "now" generation, they are, in truth, ships without a rudder, jets with no radar, missiles with no particular destination. Their experience is both good news and bad news. The good news is that they are making excellent time through life, but the bad news is that they don't know where they are going.

And so the question repeats itself: "To be or not to be?" Is it really worth it all? Can one find peace in this uncertain, confused puzzle of life? Why indeed are we here? Is there any balm in this bitter Gilead of human misery? Is there some exalted design for our existence? I hear Brother Paul saying, "Yes, life can be beautiful." There is a high and noble purpose to it all. In spite of the unsolvable circumstances, in spite of the hostile ways of nature, in spite of the treachery of humans, in spite of the Nays that tremble on our lips in the face of injustice and disappointment and what sometimes seems to be silence of an absentee God—there is hope in Jesus! He is our only Guide through the tragedy, the mystery, the cruelty, the uncertainty of life. In Him is the Yea!

But Paul's words reveal not only the fundamental tension of our existence, they also alert us to specific ways in which Christ responds to our needs.

First of all, Christ is the Yea to the *value* of life. The psalmist brings the question of value or worth to full view when he asks, "What is man, that thou art mindful of him? and the son of man, that thou visitest him?" (Psalm 8:4). Or, again, when he inquires, "Lord, what is man, that thou takest knowledge of him! or the son of man, that thou makest account of him! Man is like to vanity: his days are as a shadow that passeth away" (Psalm 144:3, 4).

What is man? In fact, not very much. Chemically analyzed, our bodies comprise approximately twelve and a half gallons of water, three and a half pounds of calcium, one-fourth ounce of iron, and one-fifth ounce of sugar. Three percent of our body weight is comprised of nitrogen, and we contain enough carbon to fill 9,000 lead pencils, enough phosphorus to make 2,000 match heads, and enough fat for seven bars of soap. Were all these ingredients mixed together, the results would look like mud. What is man? A seventy-year clock destined to expire, who, even when his days are extended, finds them to be labor and sorrow. What is man? An inconspicuous digit on nature's vast screen of eternity. What is man? A fallen prince or princess, a prodigal child confined to the husks and filth of this pigpen existence of life.

What is man? A bundle of miswired nerves, a package of diseased flesh, a carrier of infectious transgression—the inevitable result of hearts that are deceitful and desperately wicked. What is man? A creation subject to extreme paradox, in which good people suffer bad breaks and bad people often prosper, in which nice people are often abused while devious people climb to the top. Members of a society in which the best of art, science, and music goes unappreciated and the vulgar and rude are exalted and embraced. What is man? A lunatic child, a bloody monster, an embarrassment to God, a discordant note in the symphony of eternity, unworthy and unappreciative of God's love. And yet, "God so loved the world, that he gave his only begotten Son, that whosoever believeth in him should not perish, but have everlasting life" (John 3:16).

And that injection of divinity makes the difference. Through Christ, our devaluation is revalued. Our natural worthlessness is reversed toward good. Our deserved condemnation is commuted, our sentence stayed. By becoming the Son of Man, by taking on human identity, by depositing the Gem of heaven within the cesspool of humanity, Jesus has made life valuable again. Without Him, humans are the hopeless occupants of a condemned and dying commune. With Him, we become the apple of God's eye, prized and beloved, supremely valued despite our massively wretched condition.

Because the Embodiment of all value was with us; because He has become our Brother; because He walked our streets, drank our water, ate our food, breathed our air, felt our pain, bore our sorrow, carried our griefs, experienced our temptations, adopted our nature, and returned home to the Father "forever to retain His human identity," we are restored—redeemed! The incarnation changes our status from strangers to heirs, from hapless to hopeful, from global liabilities to cosmic assets. The value we now assume is not only earthly, it is universal. Like the master artist, who used the ugly blotch that his pupil had spilled upon the otherwise spotless cloth as the focal point for a stunning creation, Jesus by His life and death has made this foul planet the universal highlight of God's mercy and grace. In Him is the Yea!

But He is Yea not only to the *value* of life, He is Yea to the *purpose* of life. What is the purpose of life? The purpose of a thing is the reason for which it is made, its highest aim, its distinctive function. The function of a thing is discovered, according to Aristotle, by finding what is both common and unique to that thing. That which is common and unique to all humans is rational activity. Humans have life, but so do plants. Humans have perception, but so do beasts. What separates us from the lower forms is our rational capacity—our ability to organize data, to record facts and examine history, to utilize the raw materials of the universe for our convenience and comfort. And the most important function of rationality is the capacity of the "created" to hold communion with the "Creator." To view His handiwork and declare with David, "The heavens declare the glory of God; and the firmament sheweth his handywork," is humanity's greatest advantage over other life—the highest exercise of our rationality.

Our first parents' rational powers were energized by face-to-face communion with Him who is total intelligence, the source or dynamo of all knowledge. Sin severed that privilege. By separating us from the origin of knowing, sin became a barrier to true intellect: the Nay to knowledge, the Nay to our creation, the Nay of our purpose. By the time Jesus came, human rationality—twisted, warped, and muted by sin—was almost extinguished. It was the lack of rational capacity in that generation that the prophet described when he said: "Darkness shall cover the earth, and gross darkness the people" (Isaiah 60:2).

But when the Word became flesh and dwelt among us, He was as light shining in darkness. The presence of Christ was a contrary force to ignorance and irrationality. In Him the Yea shared through the prophets, the affirmation that had been colorfully portrayed in the sanctuary, was given its fulfillment. In Him, type met antitype. The source and dynamo of true knowledge was with us. His presence brought relief to the minds of a sick and confused society. Wherever He walked, cool glades fanned the parched vineyards of intellectual blindness and superstition.

Even more wonderful than the giving of sight to the blind, making the lame to walk, causing the deaf to hear, and freeing the tongues immobile from birth was the healing of minds crazed by sin. It was humanity's most glorious hour. The light of universal intellect was shining through the darkness of human misery. For three years, earth's inhabitants were energized by contact with God's divine/human Yea. Then when He departed, the "flesh became Word" and was embodied in the Book that He left us. Jesus was the Word reduced to flesh. The Bible is His flesh reduced to Word, and it contains the same life-giving powers that He exercised while with us.

Peter exulted in the fact that for him and the other apostles, the alienation had been broken. Once again, humanity could walk and talk with God. Through the study of the Word, we too are brought into contact with the fountain of all intelligence. Jesus Christ is heaven's Antidote to mental deficiency, the divine Reconciler of our discordant emotions and distorted reasoning, the Restoration of God's purposes for our creation. In Him is the Yea!

But Jesus is Yea not only to the *value* of life and the *purpose* of life. He is Yea to *life everlasting*. The most formidable challenge to optimism about life is the specter of death, the knowledge of our impending demise. How much easier it would be to have optimism about our existence if the grave did not yawn at the end of the road, if there were no "long home" where we all become food for worms, if there were no "mysterious realm where each shall take his chamber in the silent halls of death." The knowledge of our future nonbeing, the signs of our creeping mortality, weigh heavily against a cheerful acceptance of our tenuous existence. Too bad this journey doesn't have a happy ending, but "the living know that they shall die."

As one subject of life's inevitability said, "If I only knew where I was going to die, and when I was going to die, I just wouldn't go there at that time." But it is not a matter of "if." It's a case of "when." And Job gets to the heart of the question when he asks, "If a man die, shall he live again?"

Six thousand years of grave markers say Nay. The decayed cultures of Babylon, Greece, and Rome say Nay. The billions of princes and paupers who have marched across the stage of life in glittering array or common cloth—only to disappear forever over the dark precipice of death—say Nay. The empty chairs around the table say Nay. The physicians who sadly sew back up the irreparably ill say Nay. The pictures on the walls portraying styles and faces long departed say Nay. Each broken bone, every gray hair, each twitching nerve, and every sensation of pain cries Nay. The Nays of our reality are a formidable barrier to hope, an ever-present chorus reminding us of our mortality.

But countering all of the evidence of human history is the startling word from the angel—"He is not here: for he is risen" (Matthew 28:6). Jesus lives—He's alive! He not only overcame the formidable logistics of the incarnation, He overcame the fierce temptations of sin and the binding claims of death. Death has been swallowed up in victory; Jesus is the Yea of life everlasting!

One of the most intriguing illustrations of this latter truth is the saga of Stanley Ketchel. Ketchel was a boxer of the early twentieth century respected for his marvelous resilience. On many occasions during his long and distinguished career, he was knocked down but never knocked out. Ketchel seemed always able to get up before the referee counted to ten. He was known to "beat the count." Often apparently defeated, Ketchel would struggle to his feet and manage to win. But one night, along the back alleys of a large eastern city, Stanley Ketchel was shot and killed. The news stunned his fans, his family, and the nation. It was noted in the papers that Ketchel was finally down, and this time for good.

It so happened that Ketchel's manager was in Europe and had to be cabled the news of his death. He, of course, was devastated by the report, but he quickly gathered himself and gave to the clerk a tear-stained reply to send back across the ocean. His brief message read: "Start counting; he'll get up." The Old Testament is the promise of a Messiah, a Deliverer who would free humanity from the Nays of sin. The initial promise was, Satan shall bruise His heel, but He shall bruise Satan's head (see Genesis 3:15). Meaning? In the rescue of humanity, Christ would be painfully afflicted, while Satan would be mortally wounded. In the end, the bleeding lamb would slay the angry dragon.

Christ said of His bruise: "Destroy this temple, and in three days I will raise it up" (John 2:19). But the question after Calvary was, Could He deliver? Would His word be Yea or Nay? Was the resurrection possible? The tears of the women who anointed His body said Nay. The still form in the tomb said Nay. The stone sealing the sepulcher say Nay. The disciples, cowering in fear behind closed doors, said Nay.

It looked very bad that Friday evening when they laid His battered, broken body in the tomb. However, the Father knew that He could rely upon His Son. He knew that in Him there was life original—unborrowed and underived. Thus He could confidently say to a downcast universe: "Start counting; He'll get up!" On Friday, when the count was *one*, there was absolute stillness in the grave, and while heaven watched and disciples trembled, demons leaned nervously upon the seal of His grave. On Sabbath, the count was *two,* and there was a hushed anticipation throughout the cosmos. Could Jesus do it? He had said, "I lay down my life, that I might take it again." He had kept all other promises, but could He come back from the dead?

On Saturday evening, the count reached *three*—Jesus was still down and apparently out. Finally, the dark hours between midnight and dawn arrived. Could He get up? Would it be Yea or Nay? And then it happened! Jesus rose, not by the power of the Father nor by the voice of the angel envoy, but by the life that was in Himself. The cosmic interrogatory is answered! The plan of salvation is sealed. There is a way out for the human race.

Does God keep His word? Even when we don't understand, even when the way looks dark, even when our paths seem hedged with impossibilities, does God have a purpose and a plan? Can God help us in this mixed-up, helter-skelter tragic comedy of life? Can He give us meaning and happiness and fulfillment and purpose? The grave clothes folded neatly on the slab say Yea, the empty tomb shouts Yea, Mary running from the garden cries Yea, the Stranger who chats on the way to Emmaus says Yea. The figure on the retreating cloud says Yea. Nature says Yea. History says Yea, and, as "our faith looks up to thee, thou Lamb of Calvary," we too say Yea.

The incarnation is the Yea to the *value* of life. His Word is Yea to the *purpose* of life. His death and resurrection are Yea to *life everlasting*. The verdict is in. The matter is clear. The issue is decided. The case is closed. Christ is not Yea, Yea and Nay, Nay. In Him "is Yea—and Amen."

More than he prized his Jewish heritage or his Roman citizenship, Paul prized his place in the kingdom; not the heavenly kingdom, which he understood was future, but that of the present kingdom of grace, of which he was such a powerful proponent.

Chapter 5

This Kingdom Business

"Giving thanks unto the Father, which hath made us meet to be partakers of the inheritance of the saints in light: Who hath delivered us from the power of darkness, and hath translated us into the kingdom of his dear Son" (Colossians 1:12, 13).

Kingdom theology is not tangential to salvation. It is the fundamental framework of all Christian endeavor. It is the view which, more than any other, clarifies our relationship to our God and our responsibility to our fellow beings.

First of all, to appreciate this important concept, one must understand that the Bible outlines a number of different kingdoms. The first is the *kingdom of man*, the Eden paradise, which Adam and Eve abdicated by transgression, the utopia from which our parents, following their sin, were barred by cherubims with flaming swords.

The second kingdom of biblical account is the *kingdom of darkness*, established by Satan when Adam surrendered the authority with which he had been entrusted. Christ refers to this kingdom in Luke 11:18. And in Ephesians 6:12, Paul references this operation when he states: "We wrestle not against flesh and blood, but against principalities, against powers, against the rulers of the darkness." Ellen White linked these first two kingdoms when she wrote: "By transgression, man became his captive, and man's kingdom also was betrayed into the hands of the archrebel" *(Patriarchs and Prophets*, p. 331).

A third kingdom of importance is brought to view in Matthew 4:8: "Again, the devil taketh him up into an exceeding high mountain, and sheweth him all the kingdoms of the world, and the glory of them." The *kingdoms of the world* are the nations of the earth—the political units of humanity. Nebuchadnezzar saw them as Babylon, Medo-Persia, Greece, Rome, and the other parts of his metal image (see Daniel 2:37-44). Our Lord beheld them from the mountain as the provinces and city-states of the then-known world.

But that isn't all. Scripture tells of a fourth kingdom category. This kingdom is also described by Matthew:

> When the Son of Man shall come in his glory, and all the holy angels with him, then shall he sit upon the throne of his glory: . . . Then shall the King say unto them on his right hand, Come, ye blessed of my Father, inherit the kingdom prepared for you from the foundation of the world (Matthew 25:31-34).

This, of course, is the *kingdom of glory*—the kingdom we refer to when we pray, "Thy kingdom come," the kingdom represented as the stone that destroyed all the other kingdoms in Nebuchadnezzar's dream, the everlasting kingdom of light that Christ will institute at His return.

And so, we have them: the kingdom of man, the kingdom of Satan, the kingdoms of this world, and the kingdom of glory. But the kingdom of which Paul speaks in Colossians 1:12, 13, the kingdom of which Jesus spoke in Matthew 24:14, is none of the above. Which kingdom is it? It is the *kingdom of grace*. This is the kingdom that surfaces in Mark 1:14, 15: "Now after that John was put in prison, Jesus came into Galilee, preaching the gospel of the kingdom of God, and saying, The time is fulfilled, and the kingdom of God is at hand."

The kingdom of grace is also focused in the language of Hebrews 4:15, 16:

> We have not an high priest which cannot be touched with the feeling of our infirmities; but was in all points tempted like as we are, yet without sin. Let us therefore come boldly unto the throne of grace, that we may obtain mercy, and find grace to help in time of need.

Of course, we moderns are not as familiar with kingdom terminology as were our predecessors. In centuries past, the world was dotted with kingdom configurations. A few places still exist where royalty rule or exist in ceremonial splendor. But our primary acquaintance with kingdom traditions comes from reading history or visiting the ruins of ancient civilization, the pride of dynasties long since past. This much we do know. In each kingdom, the throne was the symbol of power, the focus of rulership, and the seat of authority. Its size, shape, and material distinguished its style of rule and typified the monarch's personality and influence. It was this focus that Paul had in mind when he spoke of the throne of grace in Hebrews 4:15, 16. Ellen White observed:

> The throne of grace represents the kingdom of grace; for the existence of a throne implies the existence of a kingdom. In many of His parables Christ uses the expression "the kingdom of heaven" to designate the work of divine grace upon the hearts of men (*The Great Controversy*, p. 347).

The kingdom of glory is the kingdom of *tomorrow*—to be inaugurated upon the return of our Lord—the physical, literal, eternal home of the redeemed. The kingdom of grace is *now*. Promised at the fall when the plan of redemption was announced, it was inaugurated by Christ upon His entrance into ministry. Of its inauguration, Dr. Luke writes: "It came to pass afterward, that he went throughout every city and village, preaching and shewing the glad tidings of the kingdom of

God: and the twelve were with him" (Luke 8:1).

The kingdom of grace is the principle of good tidings. It is the news that at Bethlehem, Christ parachuted behind the enemy lines and established in the midst of Satan's kingdom a beachhead of light. It is the excitement of knowing that the counterattack against sin has now begun, that help for humans has arrived in the person of the Messiah, that the rescue from eternal damnation has been formally launched. The great commission of Matthew 24:14 was not to center in the future kingdom of glory but in the present kingdom of grace.

The kingdom of grace occupied a more prominent place in the preaching of Jesus than any other doctrine. In fact, He mentions it in the book of Matthew alone thirty-six times— thirty-one as the kingdom of heaven and five as the kingdom of God. It was the kingdom of grace that Jesus intended when He said, "Seek ye first the kingdom of God," and, "As ye go, preach, saying, 'the kingdom of heaven is at hand.' " Unfortunately, we have been so busy emphasizing golden streets, jasper walls, and the sea of glass in the kingdom of glory that we have neglected our focus upon the important issues of the kingdom of grace.

But then, we are not the only generation that has failed to properly distinguish the kingdom of grace from the kingdom of glory. The Jewish population of Christ's generation also confused the issue. In fact, Christ had come to establish the grace era. Their mistaking those events for the glory era yet to come was the basis of their rejection of His ministry. They saw Jesus as the champion of their civil rights only. To them, His capacity to make wine out of water, to multiply fish and bread, to make blind persons see, and to calm the raging sea were signs of what could really happen if He led their armies against Rome.

And the leaders of the people, the Herodians and the Sanhedrin scholars, were no better. They read the prophecies with an eye for glory. Sure, there was a Messiah to come out of Bethlehem; sure, He would be born of a virgin. But *this* Jesus could not be the genuine article. In the first place, He was always correcting their pronouncements. In the second place, He showed absolutely no inclination for structuring the literal Davidic rule, which they longed to see restored.

Even the disciples missed the point; that's why they jostled for the highest place. It is what led the mother of James and John to request that "in the kingdom" her sons would sit one on the right and the other on the left of Christ. Inspiration records:

> With high hopes and joyful anticipations the disciples looked forward to the establishment of Messiah's kingdom at Jerusalem to rule over the whole earth. . . . From their very birth their hearts had been set upon the anticipated glory of an earthly empire, and this blinded their understanding alike to the specifications of the prophecy and to the words of Christ (*The Great Controversy*, p. 345).

The disciples never clearly understood the business of the kingdom. Proof of this is provided at the ascension of Christ, the last meeting they had with their departing Lord. Here their final question to Him was, "Lord, wilt thou at this time restore again the kingdom to Israel?" (Acts 1:6). For three years, Christ had emphasized the nature of His ministry. For three years, He had sought to help them understand the kingdom principle. In the Sermon on the Mount, He had outlined its citizenship in startling clarity. And by His life of humility and service, He had faithfully demonstrated the kingdom principle. But here at the parting they still did not conceive its true character. The Jewish population missed it. The Jewish leaders missed it. The disciples missed it, and believe it or not, we too have blurred its distinctions.

Why is it so difficult to conceive the principles of this kingdom? There are two primary reasons. First, it is natural for the human heart to yearn for the gifts of glory. Who wouldn't want to walk on golden streets within jasper walls, to eat of the tree of life and live forever in a sinless paradise with family and friends? Who wouldn't want to investigate the endless secrets of the universe and shout praise to God while following the Lamb whithersoever He goeth? The kingdom of glory has ultimate attractions for every sober, logical mind. I'd gladly trade this crime-ridden, diseased, degenerated, doomed planet for the world of light and love, wouldn't you? Of course! But the problem is that we forget that our right to life in the kingdom of glory is contingent upon our citizenship walk in the kingdom of grace. It's grace before glory, and we err when we allow the attractions of glory to preempt our interest in the principles of grace.

The second reason the kingdom of grace takes a back seat to the kingdom of glory is that the kingdom of grace functions on principles which are both contrary and painful to our ordinary way of thinking. Its rules are so foreign to human logic that Jesus had difficulty identifying earthly institutions with which to compare it. His question was, "Whereunto shall we liken the kingdom of God? or with what comparison shall we compare it?" (Mark 4:30). Then, frustrated by His search for parallels among human creations, He turned to the lesson book of nature and said, It's like the mustard seed; it's like leaven; it's like the farmer sowing; it's like the treasure hid in the field; it's like the fisherman's net; etc.

It was by these simple, everyday illustrations that Christ highlighted the grace kingdom which He came to inaugurate. By these illustrations, we are taught that the kingdom of grace is very different from the kingdoms of earth. The kingdoms of earth are physical, but the kingdom of grace is spiritual. The kingdoms of earth are visible, but the kingdom of grace is invisible. The kingdoms of earth are ushered in with much pomp and circumstance, with parades and fanfares, with celebrities and high style and great drama. But the kingdom of grace comes not with observation. It is planted in our hearts by the silent but effective movings of the Holy Spirit.

And the kingdoms differ not only in form, they also differ in terms of reward. In the kingdoms of earth, status is accorded on the basis of one's deeds, but in the kingdom of grace, it is judged on the basis of motives. In the kingdoms of earth, deference is demanded by title, but in the kingdom of grace, it is bestowed because of character. In the kingdoms of earth, it's the number that one rules that impresses, but in the kingdom of grace, it's the number that one serves.

And the kingdoms differ in terms of our citizenship relations. In the kingdoms of earth, it's "do unto others before they do unto you" and "winner take all," but in the kingdom of grace, it's "in honor preferring one another," "love your enemies, do good to them which hate you, bless them that curse you, and pray for them which despitefully use you."

And the kingdoms differ with respect to controls. In the kingdoms of earth, controls are imposed by means of legal and physical sanctions; by handcuffs and nightsticks and guns, by dogs and jails, and, finally, by firing squads, electric chairs, poisonous needles, the executioner's sword, and the hangman's noose. But in the kingdom of grace, the control is internal; it is the work of the Holy Spirit.

While many ways exist in which the principles of these two kingdoms differ, these kingdoms agree in one respect—the demand of absolute loyalty from subjects. By the rules of ancient warfare, captives whose lives were spared became grateful slaves, forever at the mercy of their captors. They owed everything to the king. They had no voting rights or land titles, and all their labors were for the benefit of the sovereign. We, like Paul, have been rescued—transplanted from the kingdom of sin and darkness into the kingdom of love and light. We are no longer our own. Our overarching responsibility is the care and upbuilding of the Master's cause, and the principles and rules of His kingdom must guide our daily priorities.

And since the kingdom of grace is contained by no physical borders, no mountains or streams or walls or fences, wherever its citizens go, they are pushing back the boundaries of its influence, extending the kingdom territory.

It was in the Garden of Eden, at the scene of the crime, that the grace kingdom was announced. But it was in A.D. 27 at the River Jordan when Christ was identified by the Baptist as the Lamb of God that the securing of the kingdom began. For three tension-filled, eventful years, Christ fought Satan in hand-to-hand combat for kingdom supremacy. His mission was not to physically eradicate the kingdom of Satan. It was rather to secure His embryonic kingdom in the lives of His followers and, from this platform of salvation, launch His offensive against the enemy. His troops were ordered to go forth, conquering in His name, and to continue until finally the kingdom principles, as demonstrated in their teaching and in their living, would either redeem or condemn the whole of humanity.

And Satan vigorously pursued his counteroffensive. First, he slaughtered all the baby boys of Judea. Then, inch by inch, step by step, Satan attempted to overwhelm and discourage Christ. It was after Christ's baptism that Satan carried Him to a high mountain in the lonely desert, where Satan made an offer he hoped Christ could not refuse. Pointing to the glittering domes and golden harvests that lay beyond, "My kingdoms for your homage," he proposed, "I'll give you all this without the pain, without Gethsemane, without the cross, if You will only fall down and worship me." Christ's immediate response was: "It is written, Thou shalt worship the Lord thy God, and him only shalt thou serve" (Matthew 4:10).

But then there was a prior question, not expressed but which Jesus also understood. These were really not Satan's kingdoms to give. True, he had wrested the keys of this domain from the grasp of Adam, but Adam was only the ethnarch of this earthly terrain. His was conditional dominion. He ruled by authority of another. Had not David said, "The earth is the Lord's, and the fulness thereof; the world, and they that dwell therein"? (Psalm 24:1). Satan, after all, was but an imposter, a created being who had laid claim to the property of the Monarch whose land it is. And besides, the agreement had been made; the only payment that God would accept for our sin was a perfect sacrifice. There could be no shortcuts for the securing of the kingdom. The prophet had said, "He shall see the travail of his soul, and shall be satisfied" (Isaiah 53:11). Jesus must pay the full price: the gift of His life as payment for our salvation.

When upon the cross He cried, "It is finished," the Roman soldiers thought Jesus meant that He was finished; the disciples thought it meant that they were finished; the Sanhedrin thought it meant that their dastardly deed was finished; the rabble thought it meant that the young church was finished; the angels thought their commander was finished. But what He meant was that His work was completed. He had, against unbelievable odds, overcome the devil; He had won the victory over temptation and discouragement and death. He had defeated the enemy on his own grounds—in his territory—and had accomplished on the cross the final act of securing the kingdom. By His death, humanity was released from the necessity of sin's servitude. When He rose, He returned to the Father with the resurrected trophies of His conquest and was formally recognized as Victor, the King whose right to rule was clearly established.

It seems only appropriate that the apostle Paul, whose kingdom imagery is so valuable in focusing this lesson, gives the benediction to our thoughts. He does so by reminding us that in the regeneration, the kingdoms of grace and glory will be united—that is, fused as one. His words are: "For this ye know, that no whoremonger, nor unclean person, nor covetous man, who is an idolater, hath any inheritance in the kingdom of Christ and of God" (Ephesians 5:5). So it is that the throne of glory will be yoked with the throne of grace, and instead of the forbidding swords of guarding angels, we will have there the beckoning lights of united kingdoms—revolving forever in harmonious praise to the Hero of our redemption, the Champion of our salvation. And, "He shall reign where 'ere sun doeth her successive journeys run, His kingdom stretch from shore to shore, 'til moon shall wax and wane no more."

The frailty of humanity was ever present to the conscience of the great apostle. Over and over again he referred to his temporary "house of flesh." The Thessalonians were also starkly aware of their human condition. This knowledge for them brought sadness and despair. For Paul, it was a reality overcome by the person and power of Christ.

Chapter 6

Treasure in Earthen Vessels

"For God, who commanded the light to shine out of darkness, hath shined in our hearts, to give the light of the knowledge of the glory of God in the face of Jesus Christ. But we have this treasure in earthen vessels, that the excellency of the power may be of God, and not of us" (2 Corinthians 4:6, 7).

Paul's analogy is rooted in one of the oldest of human crafts, that of pottery making. Recent archeological digs in the Middle East show that the potter's profession in ancient times was vital to the lifestyle and economy of ancient times. The highly diversified line of products, which researchers continue to unearth, includes bowls, buttons, candlesticks, dishes, lamps, toys, water jugs, flower vases, and other essential articles of common usage.

The object to which Paul refers in our text, the treasure chest, was particularly prized. It was a highly decorated receptacle in which the ancients placed their prized possessions and often hid in obscure places for safekeeping. Jesus Himself drew analogies from this tradition when He spoke of the farmer who stumbled upon such a box while plowing and sold all that he had in order to buy the field in which the treasure chest lay (see Matthew 13:44). It is this tradition that Paul had in mind when he states: "We have this treasure in earthen vessels."

Notice how accurately this comparison speaks to our human condition. First of all, observe that the apostle likens us to *earthen* vessels. This distinction is basic to his premise. There were many other kinds of vessels. There were vessels of gold, of silver, of brass, of stone, and of wood. In fact, the cheapest, most fragile, most expendable, least desirable of all the vessels were those made of dirt. These "clay pots" were capable of less mass, were more easily cracked, and if dropped, quickly broken. By calling us "earthen" vessels, Paul portrays as graphically as possible the fundamental frailty of humankind. He is saying that we humans are made of perishable material and that we are a fragile, transitory, earthen lot.

And consider how "earthen" we really are. Consider our physical frailty. Born as helpless babes in the blood and pain of an agonizing mother, we are welcomed to life with a stinging slap and respond with a painful scream—appropriate harbingers of the difficult experiences that lie ahead. And recall that although the birth process is but temporary trauma for most, it is a lasting tragedy for many.

But even if the process is normal and we arrive with the usual biological equipment, our mortality is immediately evidenced. For soon after birth, we are punctured with needles and made to swallow poisonous potions tempered to immunize against the bacteria which from birth vie for control of our bodies. If we are fortunate enough to survive that early process, we must still walk on polluted earth and drink polluted water, eat polluted food, breathe polluted air, and suffer the bombardment of polluted noises. And while all that is going on, we constantly live in the shadow of death by speeding autos, falling aircraft, stray bullets, and scores of other means over which we have little or no control.

And even if we escape these disasters, it is still true that "our hearts like muffled drums are beating funeral marches to the grave." We sew in the spare parts and snap on our braces and swallow our pills—the red ones, the green ones, the red and green ones, the oblong ones, the round ones, the flat ones, and the ones with all the corners. But despite our protestations, despite our attempts to reinforce our sagging anatomies, despite our multiple prescriptions, the facelifts, the hair dyes, and all the other maneuvers we employ in our struggle against death, Father Time and Mother Nature collaborate at last, enforcing our "no-moreness," and "Man goeth to his long home, and the mourners go about the streets" (Ecclesiastes 12:5). The dying bury the dead and weep over the remains of the earthen vessels who precede them in fulfillment of the curse: "Dust to dust, earth to earth, ashes to ashes."

But we are earthen, not only in terms of our physiological selves, but in our psychological makeup as well. Heredity and environment have seared us emotionally. Some authorities now agree that perhaps Freud was right after all. We do drag along the assorted baggage, the fixations we acquired during the maturation periods of childhood and youth.

Otto Rank, a contemporary of Freud, expanded upon Freud's theory by saying that we are affected by the very process of birth. Rank argued that the degree of trauma with which the individual is born establishes patterns for response to crises the rest of one's life. Some analysts say now that we are all "a little bit" insane. The difference between the majority who are free and the minority behind tall walls is one of degree. It's the radically deviant whom we institutionalize, not those of us who memorize and mimic the niceties of society. One thing is certain—we are all damaged by life. We are all projectors and protectors of the selves we fear, the manias and phobias we hide. We all must guard against being overwhelmed by the psychoses and neuroses that characterize our generation.

A psychotic is a person who interprets reality with conclusions foreign to normal perception. A neurotic is one who sees reality with perception closer to the norm but who gives exaggerated weight to its consequences. The psychotic sees that 2 plus 2 equals 5, and he could care less; while the neurotic sees 2 plus 2 equals 4, and it worries him to death. Modern society can do that to us. The very nature of our frenzied civilization, the pursuit of material gain, the concern for safety, the unrelenting quest for status and success inevitably take their toll.

We all have our inherited and cultivated idiosyncrasies. If you could only hear the rest of us talking about you when you are not around, you would understand what I mean. Everyone is a little too "something." You know how it goes: He's too loud, or he's too quiet; too accommodating or too mean; too ambitious or too lazy; too cocky or too naive; too stiff or too loose; a little too loyal or a little too independent; and so it goes. The truth of the matter is that we *are* struggling to keep our equilibrium, and we show it with our ulcers, our hypertension, our backaches, our headaches, our thrombosis, our Maalox, our Tums, our hot-water bottles, our diuretics, our "uppers" and our "downers." It should be clear that we are housed in earthen vessels.

We are also earthen spiritually. We all experience the process Freud portrays as "the distress of the ego: caught between the lusty demands of the amoral id and the repressive restraints of the moral superego," a process we know as temptation. And because we sometimes err, we are, at best, as Luther observed, "spiritual beggars"; ragged publicans beating our breasts in humble acknowledgement of our sins. Like Peter, we often "declare allegiance" but find ourselves weeping at the cock's crowing; we are like the disciples "desiring power" but sleeping in the presence of transfiguration events; we are like David "playing the fool"; Moses "smiting the rock"; and Isaiah, whose evaluation of his righteousness and ours reads "filthy rags." And the longer we are Christians, the more unworthy we see ourselves to be.

Ellen White does nothing for our egos when she writes: "The closer you come to Jesus, the more faulty you will appear in your own eyes; for your vision will be clearer, and your imperfections will be seen in broad and distinct contrast to His perfect nature" (*Steps to Christ*, p. 64).

Now if the apostle had stopped here with his assessment

of our frailty, he would have left us immersed in an inextricable dilemma. But the highlight of the story is not our earthiness, our transitoriness, the weakness of the vessel. It is our treasured possession. And what is that treasure? Is it the Sabbath, is it tithe paying, is it the church's organizational structure? These are important, but none is the treasure. What, then, is it? Verse six of 2 Corinthians 4 answers succinctly: "God, who commanded the light to shine out of darkness, hath shined in our hearts, to give the light of the knowledge of the glory of God in the face of Jesus Christ." Our treasure is the knowledge of Jesus Christ; Jesus is the Treasure who transforms the earthen vessels. Wuest's New Testament translation calls this: "An illumination being given of the knowledge of the glory of God in the face of Christ." The Living Bible reads: "The brightness of his glory that is seen in the face of Jesus Christ." The Jerusalem Bible has it: "The knowledge of God's glory, the glory on the face of Christ."

The word *knowledge* that the King James uses is translated by Luther as *erkennen*, the German word for knowing, as in having acquaintance with another human. That he utilizes *erkennen* and not *wissen*—the word for *knowing,* as in memorizing facts or numbers—is highly significant. By this choice of words, we are reminded that to have the treasure is not simply a matter of intellectual knowledge—the possession of truth as in "proof " and memorization of texts—it is rather the enjoyment of Christ's fellowship through the study of His Word. It is to know Him relationally through the living dynamics of our daily experience.

There are other treasures. *Education* is a treasure. Education, in fact, is a marvelous aid for the ennobling of humans. It will stimulate us to proper speech, it expands our world view, it raises us in social status. *Love* is a treasure. Love, that is, romantic love, will make us comb our hair and shine our shoes. It will make us brush our teeth and put a crease in our pants. Love will make a clod a gentleman and transform a tomboy into a lady. Love is a treasure. And *money* is a treasure. It will buy us a house, clothe our family, provide us an education, put us in a brand new car. And all that too is good. But there is only one treasure, one power, that can take an earthen vessel and make out of it a vehicle fit for God's approval. And that power is the knowledge of Jesus Christ.

The difference between this treasure and all others is that Jesus not only identifies our goals and stimulates our desire to achieve, He also gives us power to perform the stipulations of His commands. He provides power to grow not only in terms of cultural enhancement but to achieve spiritual victories over our carnal natures and power to witness to others as effective instruments in His cause. It is then that we become as vessels for honor, "sanctified, and meet for the master's use, and prepared unto every good work" (2 Timothy 2:21).

The Living Bible translates verse 7 of our text as saying: "This precious treasure—this light and power that now shine within us—is held in a perishable container . . . [so] that the glorious power within must be from God." Yes, *all* credit for success in divine operations belongs to God. This does not make human agency unessential, but it is clearly non-determinative—the power is of God. It was so with the apostles, it was so with the reformers, it was so with our pioneers, and it is so with us. The results we achieve must never be attributed to feeble instrumentality; the answer to our successes is the power of God, not our strength or genius. Furthermore, the weaker the vessel, the more obviously God's participation is seen.

During my presidency at Oakwood College, I often had occasion to visit churches, where I took pride in "selling" the school. While detailing accomplishments during a Sabbath worship service in Chicago, I noticed a lady acquaintance shaking her head in amazement. Chatting after the service, I asked her why she appeared so surprised at the good reports. Instead of answering immediately, she inquired of several mutual friends, asking how things were going in their areas of labor. As I gave enthusiastic information about all of them, she again expressed incredulity, slowly shaking her head in wonder. Finally she said, "You know, I can't understand it!

With all the numskulls running the work, it's a wonder things go so well. It must be the Lord." I had not expected that.

Back home I told my wife about the experience and reached out for some sympathy and consolation. "Clara," I said, "that woman called us all numskulls." Her reply was, "Well, I've been telling you that all the time." And it is probably true. But then I remembered the lesson of our text and the fact that the weaker the creature, the more obvious will be the Creator. God's chosen have often looked feeble and even foolish before overwhelming difficulties. They must have looked rather hopeless, those 300 men with Gideon who lapped water from the pond. That was a strange ragtag army of aliens blowing horns while tramping around the walls of Jericho. It was just one queer prophet on Mount Carmel dueling with 450 soldiers of Baal. And those were strange and stubborn youth who stood before Nebuchadnezzar's image when all other citizens bowed to the ground. And he had to be weak of body and reason, that little fellow confronting big Goliath with but a slingshot and some stones. And weren't they irrational, those people waiting in the upper room, praying for power to revolutionize the world? But that's the way God likes it. The longer the odds, the greater the improbability, the clearer it will be seen that the credit belongs to God.

Two thousand years ago, a voice was heard in heaven saying, "Father, a body Thou hast prepared for me," and Jesus came as heaven's Treasure, wrapped in an earthen vessel. He was here, this Treasure, in our kind of body. He was here, but they did not recognize Him:

> They knew not that that shelterless Man owned all the mansions in which the hierarchs of heaven have their habitation. They knew not that he who cried: "I thirst!" poured the Euphrates from his own chalice. They knew not that that hungered man owned all the olive gardens and all the harvests that shook their gold on the hills of Palestine. They knew not that the worlds that lighted up the Eastern night were only the glittering belt with which he clasped the robes of his glory. They knew

not that the ocean lay in the palm of his hand like a dew-drop in the vase of a lily. They knew not that all the splendors of noon-day were only the shadow of his throne. They knew not that suns, and moons, and stars, and galaxies, marching on for ages in cohorts of light, as compared with Christ's lifetime, were less than a sparkle of a fire-fly on a summer's night. . . . Eternal harmonies subdued into a human voice! Honor cloaked in shame! The crown of universal dominion covered up by a bunch of thorns! The royalty of heaven passing in earthly disguise! (Thomas DeWitt Talmage, *Traps for Men* [Fairbanks and Company, 1878], p. 122).

To those who failed to recognize Him or who realized His person but refused Him entrance, He became a "stone of stumbling"—the God of vengeance and death. But to those who received Him, He was transforming power—the revealing of creatures devalued by sin. It was true of them as it is of us that the more fully one opens up to the Treasure, the more radiant and powerful the possession. John's more extensive use of Christ was not an accident or an arbitrary bestowal; rather, John pressed closest to Jesus and "is distinguished as the one whom Jesus loved. The Saviour loved them all, but John's was the most receptive spirit" (*The Desire of Ages*, p. 292). In retrospect, he testified that he received of Christ's fullness—"grace for grace." The result was the closest fellowship and the broadest ministry granted to the Twelve.

And so we must position ourselves today—earthen vessels who open wide for the infilling of the glory of God. The more we let that infilling happen, the more will be the capacity for our containment. Should we live to welcome His soon return, He will identify us as His own. He will gather us as His jewels from the four corners of the earth, mortal, but shining with the radiance of His presence,

And should we, like John and his brethren, lie down in death to await that glad event, we will do so knowing that for us, eternity is assured, that in our dusty tombs will reside treasure in earthen vessels. If we must die, we will do so knowing that as the springtime sun brings forth life from slumbering seeds, so shall the Sun of Righteousness call forth His own to life everlasting and present us to the Father—no more earthen but celestial vessels, infinitely valued, forever redeemed.

As humans, there is much that we cannot know or answer regarding the details of Christ's kingdom or His coming. Even Paul admitted gaps in his comprehension of these matters. The move from the visible to the invisible, which faith must make, is not easy, but it is necessary.

Chapter 7

From Visible Nothing To Invisible Something

"For our light affliction, which is but for a moment, worketh for us a far more exceeding and eternal weight of glory; while we look not at the things which are seen, but at the things which are not seen: for the things which are seen are temporal; but the things which are not seen are eternal" *(2 Corinthians 4:17, 18).*

Our text finds Paul in a pensive mood. It must have been a gray day, a day when the clouds obscured the sun and nature was brooding, a day for meditation and introspection. And there by the fireplace, perhaps in his robe and favorite rocker, the apostle reminisces over the past, thumbing through the chapters of his long and exciting career. As he relives the highlights of yesteryear, he notes, among other milestones, the harsh sufferings, the painful experiences that he had encountered. Then, comparing the difficulties of that service to eternal reward, he concludes that the afflictions of the here and now are not comparable to the transcendent glory of the bliss to come. And he sums up his musings by observing that Christians are those who focus not upon the transitory difficulties of the visible universe but upon the unseen realities of the eternal tomorrow. In other words, Christians are willing to transfer their allegiance from the visible nothing of this world to the invisible something of the world to come.

We all can focus upon the visible reality about us. It is tangible; it is concrete; it is available to our senses. One of the more helpful statements of this principle was given by René Descartes, French philosopher and mathematician, who said, "I think, therefore I am." Descartes was correct. We *are* here! And there is no need for faith regarding what our senses verify. What we can touch, we can know. Our tangible existence is not an act of faith. It is a matter of fact, a demonstrable reality.

And yet, in the highest sense, the material things that we see and touch are not *true* reality. They are philosophically a "nothing." Why? Because they lack "ever-presentness." Anything qualifies as nothing if there was a time when it did not exist and if there is a time in the future when it will not be. Such matter falls under Augustine's perceptive definition: "for anything, whatsoever in short be its excellence, if it is changeable, does not truly exist; for there is no true existence wherever non-existence has also a place" (*Augustine: A Collection of Critical Essays*, ed. R. A. Markus, p. 270).

Viewed thusly, our most valued possessions are nothings. They are objects of wood or cloth or metal, pulled from the soil, sheared from animals, or spliced together by inventive humans, which—if I read my Bible correctly—will someday melt with fervent heat. They will be no more. Our most prized materials are nothings. Time itself is a nothing. It is simply the space between the eternities—eternity past and eternity future. Before sin, there was no need to count heartbeats and sunsets; there was no temporal sequence. The universe was functioning, not on clocks and measurable palpitations, but in the atmosphere of an immortality that has no beginning and no end. There was a time when there was no time, and since upon His return, time shall be no more, time is also a temporary function. It is also a nothing.

And if you want to know the truth, you and I are nothings.

Isn't that what David was trying to tell us when he said humanity is like the grass: "In the morning it flourisheth, and groweth up; in the evening it is cut down, and withereth" (Psalm 90:6)? Isn't that what James was expressing when he likened our existence to vapors, mere clouds, that evaporate into the nothingness that we were before birth (see James 4:14)? Think of how long the world was in existence before we arrived. Contemplate how short is the distance of our little journey on this planet. No matter how rich or popular we are, when we leave, we are soon forgotten: a statistic in the daily news, another cell in the massive body of humanity quickly removed from sight and replaced by other human cells, also born to die. And so the cycle continues in mortal succession—we are nothings!

But heaven, oh heaven, is a "something." It qualifies as a something because it possesses what nothingness lacks, that is, everlastingness. In the words of Peter, heaven is "an inheritance incorruptible, and undefiled, and that fadeth not away" (1 Peter 1:4). But the problem is that it is invisible. We cannot see it. It is, therefore, an *invisible* something. And that is the crux of Paul's dilemma—and ours! We must choose between a present, visible nothing and a promised, invisible something; between the natural, which we can comprehend, and the supernatural, which our senses cannot appropriate; between the phenomenal and the noumenal; between the transitory and the transcendent; between the now and the hereafter; between sight and faith; between this visible nothing and that invisible something.

And what a paradox that is! It is, in fact, a double paradox. We Christians must not only look at what we cannot see, we must believe in what we cannot understand. What does it mean to look at what one cannot see? First Corinthians 2:14 explains by affirming that spiritual things are "spiritually discerned." It is not with the physical eye that we see the invisible. We see with our spiritual eyesight, that which Ellen White calls "sanctified reason." Niebuhr terms it "internal revelation," the sight that is grounded upon trust, not demonstration.

The power to see the invisible does not come naturally to humans. We are not born with a built-in "belief structure." Faith is not a part of our original equipment. That is what Paul meant when he wrote that "the natural man receiveth not the things of the Spirit of God" (1 Corinthians 2:14). Seeing the invisible is a capacity that is awakened and developed by the study of God's Word. The life-giving, soul-quickening power of the Bible, planted in the heart by the Holy Spirit, produces for the hearer a new thing, a divine power, which appropriates for the soul what the body cannot sense. The author of Hebrews describes one of history's most celebrated examples of this phenomenon when he said of Moses: "By faith he forsook Egypt, not fearing the wrath of the king: for he endured, as seeing him who is invisible" (Hebrews 11:27).

But we Christians are mandated not only to look at what we cannot see but to believe in what we cannot understand. Augustine defines understanding as an awareness of logical necessity. Kant regarded understanding as having common root with sensibility, or, to put it another way, a matter of apprehension made possible by the functioning of the five senses. Both were right, and both highlight the difficulty of assent with respect to God. It is not easy to believe that which our senses do not grasp, that which runs contrary to our cognitive categories of time, space, color, taste, and density. We don't understand how the dead will be raised from the dust or how, given a round world, "Every eye shall see Him." We can't understand how everlastingness is possible or what omnipresence is. And we don't know how God the Son was compressed into Mary's womb—of necessity all God and all man at the same time. We do not understand, but we do believe. We surrender to what we cannot prove, cannot explain, and do not understand. It is truthfully said of the incarnation—that linchpin of all our faith—that "if you try to understand it, you lose your mind, and if you don't believe it, you lose your soul." That is the nature, yea, the crux of our faith.

Some theorists, including Augustine, taught that understanding is the superior event, and that belief is but a preliminary step to apprehension. Others, such as Aquinas, taught that belief is the higher function and that understanding or logical demonstration is preliminary to assent. But with Christ it was neither "believe to understand" nor "understand to believe." His message to Thomas and to us is: Believe even though you do not understand (see John 20:29)!

But again, given our definitions, is that possible? How can one have more confidence in a proposition than its statable grounds can logically justify? We can do so because our belief is secured, not by proofs and promises, but by testimony of the One whom we love and trust, One whose word has always proven true, One whose companionship nurtures our lives and gives meaning to our actions.

Relational theology is involved here, and evidence of the changes in our once sin-drenched lives serves as the greatest assurance that He is true, that we are not mistaken in our ultimate conclusions. What before conversion seemed incomprehensible and foolish becomes eloquent reality. All our thinking is conditioned by our association with Him. And because that association visibly ennobles and satisfies, we gladly take the risk of faith and freely choose to believe. The answer to looking at what we cannot see is *faith sight*. The answer to believing what we cannot understand is *faith knowledge*. And by these means and these alone are we enabled to turn from the visible nothing of this life to the invisible something of the life to come.

And what are the practical results of our rejecting the nothingness of this world and placing all our hopes on the something of tomorrow? First of all, such a move provides logical structure to our world view. To accept God's somethingness is to accept the doctrine of creation, to believe that "in the beginning God created the heaven and the earth" (Genesis 1:1), that we are descendants, not of tadpoles or hairy apes, but of beings created in the image of God. It is to accept the biblical account of history. It is to believe that above the din of human devisings a wise and knowing God with a loving heart yearns for sinners and rejoices over saints. It is to know that this little sin-cursed world is the one sheep that strayed when all others stayed and that Jesus is the Good Shepherd who gave His live that we might be redeemed.

Second, the move to somethingness tempers our theologizing. When challenged as to why he sought to eliminate all the standard arguments for proof of God, Kant replied, "I have taken away reason in order to establish faith." If by reason Kant meant the logic of inference, he was wrong. But if by reason he meant firm equations of certitude, he was right. Human beings, even the converted kind, cannot penetrate the cognitive barrier that separates the finite from the infinite. Not only do humans lack the equipment to locate and enter heaven, we do not have the apparatus to understand it, could we enter there.

How dare we then absolutize the representations of Scripture? With what right do we dogmatize regarding God's essence and being? The Bible is God's way of telling us in our language that we can understand enough about Him to demonstrate His love and care. It is not a lexicon, a blueprint, or a manual that details divinity. God's ethical characteristics are made clear in His Word—His goodness, His patience, and His love. And His instructions regarding our relationship to Him are also clear: "Thou shalt have no other gods before me," "thou shalt not take the name of the Lord thy God in vain," and "remember the Sabbath day, to keep it holy." But the possibility for comprehending His essence is not acquired by Bible study. We are locked out from knowing the transcendent.

Niebuhr was never more correct than when he stated, regarding our debates on divine mysteries, "Before God we are all wrong!" The move to somethingness permits us to relax our theological prattlings, to see the Bible as the story of salvation and guide to living, not the code with which we can unscramble the mysteries of divinity.

The third benefit gained from the move to somethingness is the proper ordering of our priorities. When we set our affections on things above, when the visible world is given its rightful place in relation to eternity, when the decision is made that we must reach heaven at all costs, when earthly joys fade and heavenly bliss occupies our thoughts, it shows in our lifestyle. We live differently when we latch on to somethingness than when we were fastened to nothingness. Somethingness dictates a special agenda. It tells us how to eat and what to read, who to marry, where to work. It tells us how to spend our money, where to spend our time, where to go to school. It conditions us under persecution and makes us love everybody. And it provides an experience so warm, so satisfying, that, in the words of the song, "We just can't keep it to ourselves." We are like the blind man whom Jesus healed that sunlit Sabbath. When our eyes are open to the joys of the new agenda that Christ provides, we become irrepressible witnesses of His love.

Six thousand years ago, God made something from nothing. Adam in clay form looked like something because he was shaped in the image of God. In fact, he was nothing until God breathed into his nostrils the breath of life. The breath of eternity that was transferred from God's being into the clay form made it something. But Adam's was a conditional something, a provisional eternity. Sin canceled his "somethingness." Adam's transgression resulted in the plunge from the somethingness of conditional immortality to the nothingness of death. And, because of his sin, the blight of nothingness settled upon all of creation: vegetation decayed, the elements contorted, the animals snarled, and the once-fertile soil rebelled at Adam's touch, demanding for satisfaction the sweat of his brow. With sin, death began its awesome rule, and earth's somethingness was consigned back to the dusty void from which it was created.

But God had a reserve plan, an emergency exit already in place, a way to reclaim humans, to arrest our return to oblivion. And what was that? He sent into our midst the best Something He had—His only Son Jesus. And in the fullness of time, He came. The Commander of angels condescended and tabernacled among us. He didn't stay long, but while here, He was a living dynamo of life and energy. All who touched Him revived. He wasn't just a something. He was something special. Those who came to trap Him left saying, "Never a man spake like this Man," and those who watched Him closest testified that so powerful were His words that hurricanes hushed howling at His command. No wonder Satan hated Him; no wonder He inspired unscrupulous men to dog His path till at last they effected His betrayal and trial and crucifixion.

But that was not a *conditional* something on the cross. It was *Absolute* Something—the Creator God. And you can't kill permanence. It is impossible to extinguish the eternal flame of Deity. How does one zap eternity? Jesus rose from the grave, and when He did, He turned what Satan intended as an eternal sleep into a Sabbath of rest. And as He arose, He declared the temporariness of dying and the death of death. Announcing its final nothingness, He cried, "O death, where is thy sting? O grave, where is thy victory?" Then He sealed our somethingness by declaring, "Father, thou in me and I in them." It is that which gives us hope. It is that which transforms our miserable nothingness into the glorious something that is the likeness of God.

While the saints lack final proof for many of their beliefs, they do possess overwhelming evidence. That evidence is found more than anywhere else in the life and person of Jesus Christ. Because of that assurance, Paul acquired a faith that withstood even the sentence of death.

Chapter 8

A Matter of Confidence

"Cast not away therefore your confidence, which hath great recompense of reward. For ye have need of patience, that, after ye have done the will of God, ye might receive the promise" (Hebrews 10:35, 36).

One of the core elements of the Christian experience is our 2,000-year wait on Christ's return. Did not He pledge, "If I go . . . I will come again" (John 14:3)? Did not the heavenly escorts who accompanied Him say, "This same Jesus, which is taken up from you into heaven, shall so come in like manner" (Acts 1:11)? True, He warned us of a lengthy time when He spoke of taking a *far* journey (see Mark 13:34), but the question that every longing, praying, hoping, working generation of Christians since that time has asked is, "How far?" or "How long, O Lord, how long?"

We who live today answer, "Surely not long." We see the signs! We see them in the increase of crime, of mental disorders, of crumbling ethics, and rampant immorality in the *social* world. We see them in violent eruptions of earth and sea and the clutter and cloud of poisonous wastes that defile the ecology of the *natural* world. We see them in the bloody confrontations of the *political* world—confrontations so numer-

66

ous, so varied, that we are forced to define new categories of conflict. To the standard designations of land wars, race wars, and civil wars, we have now added those of oil wars, rice wars, germ wars, drug wars, and Star Wars—all harbingers of the approaching end. And we see the signs in the dwindling spirituality: the doctrinal pollutions, the rapid escalation of papal authority, and the ecumenical alliances of the *religious* world.

But, on the other hand, our certainty is no more firm or fervent than that which was expressed in the eighties, the decade of terrorism; or the seventies at the height of the cold war; or the sixties during the worst of racial rioting; or the fifties when the space age was born; or the forties during the calamities of World War II; or the thirties during the worst of the depression; or the twenties as the nations recovered from World War I. In fact, we are no more hopeful than Brother Paul, who, living in the very shadow of the cross, wrote, "We which are alive and remain unto the coming of the Lord shall not prevent them which are asleep" (1 Thessalonians 4:15).

A review of one or two second-century commentaries on the second advent illuminates the point. We have, for example, the words of Bishop Clement, overseer in Rome in the middle of the first century, who wrote in a letter to the church at Corinth:

> "Of a truth, soon and suddenly shall His will be ac-
> complished, as the Scripture also bears witness, saying,
> 'Speedily will He come, and will not tarry;' and, 'The
> Lord shall suddenly come to His temple, even the Holy
> One, for whom ye look' " (L. E. Froom, *Prophetic Faith of
> Our Fathers*, vol. 1, p. 208).

And we have the witness of Saint Ignatius of Antioch, believed to have been a martyr in A.D. 107 during the reign of Emperor Trojan. Ignatius wrote in his epistle to the Ephesians, "The last things are upon us, let us therefore be of a reverent spirit and fear the long-suffering God that it tend not to our condemnation." Also in a letter to his good friend,

Polycarp, he advised: "Weigh carefully the times, look for Him who is above all time eternal and invisible, yet who became visible for our sakes."

Others from this early period whose expressions of apocalyptic expectations have survived include Barnabas, who, as early as A.D. 150, linked the second coming with the image of Daniel 2; Hermus, who wrote a book titled *The Shepherd of Hermus*, which is very much like the book of Revelation; Polycarp, bishop of Smyrna, believed by scholars to have been a personal friend of John the Beloved; and Papius, whose works were lost but whose beliefs about the millennium are quoted by other writers, are all penmen of this early era who pointed to an imminent return.

During the age of the apologists, A.D. 150–325, which followed the time of the New Testament church, the church suffered merciless persecutions. Among the defenders or apologists of the faith of this era whose witness regarding the end survives are Justin Martyr; Irenaeus, bishop of Lyons; Hippolytus, bishop of Rome; the two great Carthaginian church leaders, Turtulien and Cyprien; and Jerome, the Roman Christian, who taught that Rome would fall and fragment into ten pieces as symbolized by the toes of the metallic man in Nebuchadnezzar's dream (see Daniel 2).

One author of this era, Theodoret, the Greek theologian, correctly identified Christ as the stone of Daniel 2. His words are:

"If therefore the first coming of the Lord did not overthrow the empire of the Romans, it properly remains that we should understand [by this] His second advent. For the stone which was cut out before without hands, and which grew into a great mountain and covered the whole earth, this at the second advent shall smite the image upon the feet of clay" (*ibid.*, p. 452).

The period of the apologists was followed by the Dark Ages. The church began this lengthy era with great anxiety over the failure of Christ to appear at the collapse of Rome in A.D. 476. The fall of Rome had been regarded by the believers as the final sign of Christ's return, and when that did not prove true, a backlash of apathy developed. This reaction was the beginning of centuries of diminished enthusiasm regarding the second coming. That apathy did not lift until around A.D. 1000. Renewed interest in Christ's return was inspired by the realization that the millennium begun with the birth of Christ was about to end and by the hope that the Lord would mark His return with final judgments. The conquest of Jerusalem in 1009 and the terrible famines of Europe in 1033 agitated greatly this heightening expectation.

When the Reformation dawned during the latter stages of the Dark Ages, expectations of the second coming were again revived. Wycliffe, the morning star of that awakening, spoke of the Redeemer's appearing as "the hope of the church." Milic, who was impressed by the 1,335-day prophecy of Daniel 12, taught that Christ would appear 1,335 days after the crucifixion, or somewhere between 1363 and 1367. Melanchthon said, "This aged world is not far from its end"; John Calvin said, "Christians must not hesitate, ardently desiring the day of Christ's coming as of all events most auspicious"; Knox said, "We know that He shall return with expedition"; Ridley said, "The world without doubt, this I do believe and therefore say, draws to an end"; Luther said, "I will not permit anyone to rob me of my opinion that the day of the Lord is not far hence. This conviction is forced upon me by the signs that I see."

Savonarola of Italy, another Reformer who preached the apocalypse, dated his "prophetic testimony" from 1492, predicting that the sword of the Lord would descend suddenly and quickly upon the earth. This and similar preaching earned him the wrath of Rome. Consequently, he was excommunicated in 1497, imprisoned, and condemned to die on May 23, 1498. The death sentence was read to Savonarola, as he stood with bare feet and hands bound, before the bishop of Vasona, who said: "I separate thee Savonarola from the church militant and the church triumphant." "Ah-h-h, not the church triumphant," said the courageous Savonarola, "that is not thy power to do." Shortly thereafter, he and his two disciples were hanged, their bodies burned, and their ashes cast into the nearby Arno River.

Reformation expectations regarding the second coming are further illustrated by a brief look at what went on in England about this time. Titles of Christian books in the 1600s include: *The Second Coming of Christ*, by Thomas Rogers; *A Fruitful Dialogue Concerning the End of the World*, by William Perkins; *The Saints Everlasting Rest*, by Richard Baxter; and many others. Thomas Adams, who wrote in the early part of the seventeenth century, stated:

> "Deepe are we fallen into the latter end of these last dayes, that (for ought we know) before we depart this place, we may looke for the last fire to flash in our faces. We are they, upon whom the ends of the world have come" (Bryan W. Ball, *A Great Expectation*, p. 43).

A contemporary, Thomas Hall, wrote: " . . . the dayes we live in, are the last days. Our times are the last times. . . . This is the last hour . . . and upon us the ends of the world is come" (*ibid.*, p. 41).

Joseph Hall, Anglican prelate, wrote: " . . . the world is near to it's last period; and . . . our Lord Jesus is at hand, for his finall judgment. For if in the time of the blessed Apostles, it was justly computed to be the last houre, needs must it now be drawing towards the last minute" (*ibid.*, p. 163).

Even the poets got in on the action. George Wither wrote in 1625, "God's patience is nigh out of date" (*ibid.*, p. 89). And then he added:

> Be patient therefore ye that are opprest;
> This generation shall not pass away
> Till some behold the downfall of that Beast,
> Which yet upon us with his Taile doth play.
> . . . .
> I see it plainly as I see the Sun,
> He draweth near who on the white Horse rides,

The Long expected Battel is begun (*ibid.*, p. 90).

And the renowned John Milton stated in his works on the Psalms: "Surely to such as do Him fear Salvation is at hand And glory shall ere long appear To dwell within our land" (*ibid.,* p. 89).

My own favorite quotation from this period of English history is that of Henry Symons, who said:

> ". . . it will not be long before this Judge comes, though I dare not say with Alsted in his Chronol. that 1657 should be the yeare, . . . nor yet with Napier that 1688 shal be the year, . . . yet I may say with Bucanon, if 1660 yeares agoe were ultimum tempus, that then this is ultimum temporis. I may say with Tertullian, this is clausulum seculi: with Austin, Christ is in proximo: with Cyprian, he is supra caput; yea, I may say of some here as was said of Simeon, they shall not depart this life before they shall see the Lord's Christ . . . he is on the wing, he comes post, he will be here before most are aware" (*ibid.,* pp. 41, 42).

While all this was going on in Europe far across the ocean, America was gradually being populated. The Presbyterians, Congregationalists, Baptists, Episcopalians, and other denominations and sects who first settled here differed in matters like the Lord's Supper, the ministry of Christ, and baptism, but they showed remarkable unity in belief of an approaching judgment and the second coming.

Leroy Froom lists the names of no less than forty-three people whom he calls principal American exponents of prophecy during the 1600s and 1700s, or the first two centuries of America's founding (*The Prophetic Faith of Our Fathers*, vol. 3, pp. 252, 253). Chief among these are John Cotton, Roger Williams, Samuel Sewell, Jonathan Edwards, Aaron Burr, and, of course, the great Mather dynasty of revival preachers. Froom records no less than ten of these as calculating the end of the world between 1655-1890. And numerous natural disasters and military conflagrations during this period served to reinforce their prophetic calculations. These included the Lisbon earthquake in November 1755; the dark day of May 1780; the capture of the pope by the French General Berthier in 1798; and the American Revolutionary War. So impressive were these signs, so certain were the believers that the stone was about to roll upon the feet of the image that in 1757 Aaron Burr could, with conviction, write: "My Brethren, tho' we may be entering on the darkest, and the most gloomy Part of the Night, which has continued so long, we may lift up our Heads with Joy, our Salvation draws near. The *Night is far spent, and the Day is at Hand*" (L. E. Froom, vol. 3, p. 200).

As has been noted, the main springboards for prophetic calculation prior to this time had been Daniel, chapters 2 to 7. However, in the latter 1700s and early 1800s, interest in both Europe and America swung heavily to the prophecy that was to become the main axis of a group which in 1861 took on the name Seventh-day Adventists. The prophecy? The 2,300-day prophecy of Daniel 8:14. Thus, in Europe, Thomas Parker projected that the 2,300 days would end in 1649; William Burnet said that it would end in 1745; John Adams calculated the 2,300 days as ending in 1843; L. H. Kelber, in 1843. So certain was William Cummins Davis, prominent American preacher of the early 1800s, that the 2,300-day prophecy would conclude with the coming of Christ in 1847 that in 1811 he wrote the following poem:

> In forty seven we may hope
> To find the world without a Pope;
> When thirty more expel the evil,
> We'll find the world without a Devil;
> Add three years more and forty two,
> We'll find the world without a Jew:
> The Pope, and Devil, known no more;
> Until the thousand years are o'er;
> And Jew and Gentile now the same,
> Rejoice to wear the Christian name:

> The glorious dawn of forty seven,
> Will introduce new earth and heaven.
> (*ibid.*, vol. 4, p. 222).

Again, Froom lists in volume 4, page 404, a total of eighty-eight sources, which, prior to William Miller, set the terminal date of the 2,300 days between 1843 and 1847.

Of special note in this regard are the avid expectations of the Millerite movement in 1843 and 1844. Nor can we forget the many predictions of Ellen White, who spoke often and convincingly of Christ's imminent return. One of her most definitive predictions, given in May 1856, is: "I saw that some of those present would be food for worms, some subjects for the seven last plagues, and some would be translated to heaven at the second coming of Christ, without seeing death" (*Spiritual Gifts*, vol. 2, p. 208).

But it has not happened. How do we explain it to the world? How do we explain it to our children? How do we explain it to ourselves? How do we retain our confidence in the face of the grim reality of the passing centuries, the lengthening space between promise and fulfillment, the increasing likelihood that we too will join the long line of departed saints who silently wait for the blessed hope? I wish to support several of the many possible answers.

First of all, it is necessary for the Christian to remember that God's view of time is not ours. In fact, for Him, there is no time—only eternity. A thousand years are for Him "but as yesterday," and a millennium of millenniums less than the flash of energy that lightens the darkened horizon on a stormy night. We cannot chafe at the timetable of Omnipotence. We do not speak in the language of eternity, nor do we comprehend the category of everlastingness.

Second, since all humans die soon—too soon, compared to the life spans of original humans—and since the first order of business for each resurrected person will be the judgment of God and since that event (the resurrection) follows death as our morning awakening follows our night of sleep, Christ is indeed coming soon and suddenly for all of us.

Third, it is important to remember that all of God's promises are conditional. Ellen White, who spoke so confidently of an immediate return, also said:

> For forty years did unbelief, murmuring, and rebellion shut out ancient Israel from the land of Canaan. The same sins have delayed the entrance of modern Israel into the heavenly Canaan. In neither case were the promises of God at fault. It is the unbelief, the worldliness, unconsecration, and strife among the Lord's professed people that have kept us in this world of sin and sorrow so many years (*Evangelism*, p. 696).

The fact that Christ has not come is an indictment of neither the prophet nor the God of inspiration. It is rather a commentary upon the failure of the church to reflect the images that are required for final victory. The Word of God is clear: "If ye be willing and obedient, ye shall eat the good of the land" (Isaiah 1:19). "If my people, which are called by my name, shall humble themselves, . . . then will I hear from heaven" (2 Chronicles 7:14). "If thou shalt hearken diligently unto the voice of the Lord thy God, to observe and to do all his commandments . . . blessed shalt thou be in the city, and blessed shalt thou be in the field" (Deuteronomy 28:1, 3). "If thou draw out thy soul to the hungry, and satisfy the afflicted soul; then shall thy light rise in obscurity, and thy darkness be as the noon day" (Isaiah 58:10). "If thou turn away thy foot from the sabbath, . . . then shalt thou delight thyself in the Lord" (Isaiah 58:13, 14). And, "If any man hear my voice, and open the door, I will come in to him, and will sup with him, and he with me" (Revelation 3:20).

No promise, including that of the second coming, should be read without understanding that divine intention is indeed affected by human response. It is a fact that disobedience has often cancelled promised blessings. It is also a fact that repentance and obedience have reversed promised curses. God does not and cannot change His character, His personality, or His desires for our good. But, clearly, He has often changed His methodology in the conduct of His will.

Fourth, continued study of the Word of God promotes a quality of faith that provides the believer undying hope in spite of delay. Such hope prevents all possibilities of discouragement by surrendering so fully to God's will that it transcends death, viewing the grave itself as but a brief rest from which the redeemed shall shortly awaken to see their King. This is precisely the faith that Job displayed when he exclaimed:

> I know that my redeemer liveth, and that he shall stand at the latter day upon the earth: and though after my skin worms destroy this body, yet in my flesh shall I see God: whom I shall see for myself, and mine eyes shall behold, and not another; though my reins be consumed within me (Job 19:25-27).

One of my favorite illustrations of this truth is the story of the two boys who were standing in front of an abandoned cave daring one another to venture beyond its dark, foreboding entrance. "Go on in," the older said to the younger. "Don't be afraid. See, somebody else has already done it. Look right over there. I see foot tracks going in." To which the younger lad replied, "I know, and that's what's worrying me. I see tracks going in, but I don't see any tracks coming out!"

The critical difference between believers and skeptics is that the latter see Joseph's new tomb as a one-way street. There are tracks going in, but none coming out. But Christians whose minds have been quickened by the Holy Spirit are able to believe. For them, the stone is rolled away, they see the grave clothes placed neatly to the side, they see tracks going in, and they see tracks coming out. The skeptic peers into the grave that awaits him and sadly quivers, "Nothing else." The Christian looks beyond the grave and triumphantly proclaims, "There is more, much more on the other side." The skeptic says, "We are dying, we are hopelessly perishing." The Christian says, "We are being saved, made alive by Jesus Christ." The skeptic looks upon our gospel and says with

Marx, "It is the opiate of the masses." The Christian sings, "The world says I'm dreaming, but if I am dreaming, then let me dream on." The confused sufferer inquires with Job, "If a man dies, will he live again?" And Jesus, from the portals of glory responds, "I am the resurrection, and the life: he that believeth in me, though he were dead, yet shall he live" (John 11:25).

And that, ladies and gentlemen, is good enough for us. We need no dramatic pronouncements. True, "we see through a glass darkly." But we do see! We are not certain about all the mysteries of our redemption, but we see in the changes God has wrought in us that we have been and are being redeemed. We are not certain about all the details of the second coming. But we see in the prophecies that are being fulfilled with ever-increasing intensity why He must and shall return. We do not know how decayed flesh and rotted bones can be brought back to life again. But in the life that bursts forth from buried seeds we see what Ricoeur referred to as the great "as if" of nature. We see it with the eye of faith, and we dare not violate faith's boundaries by demanding more for its support than its function allows.

And so we live out our days as trusting, working, praying pilgrims in search of a better city. We move ever forward in faith, marching courageously from shadow to fulfillment, from the proximate to the ultimate, from the already to the not-yet! No, we cannot prove that Christ's return is imminent or know precisely when it will be. But we can and do hope that this time the signs are final, that He who shall come, will come— and *in our day*. We continue to believe that the unspeakable glory of His return, which all ages of Christians sought but did not experience, can be ours. We believe that for all the reasons mentioned above and more, if He does permit us to die, as have our predecessors in faith, He can and will resurrect us at the end of the age.

Our faith in these events is anchored, not in dates or in signs or in fossils, but in His matchless love. We believe in Him because we love Him, and we love Him because we have found Him to be impeccably dependable. His compassion manifested on Calvary is the guarantee of His Word. We require no other proof. And why should we? For in the final analysis, our belief is not a matter of scientific verification or technological demonstration. It is now, it has always been, and until He comes, must remain, a matter of confidence!

*The challenge of extended
expectation is always difficult.
Fortunately the early church had
the disciples, as well as Paul and
the other apostles, whose words
and presence brought them
reassurance. We too have been
waiting. We too have the presence
of the prophets and pioneers.*

Chapter 9

Christ Our Passover

**"Purge out therefore the old leaven, that ye may be
a new lump, as ye are unleavened. For even Christ
our passover is sacrificed for us" (1 Corinthians
5:7).**

It is difficult to think of a more appropriate prefix for the
title of Israel's night of deliverance than—*pass-over*. Not only
did the death angel pass over their dwellings; they passed out
of Egypt, they "passed over Jordan," they passed from cult-
hood to nationhood, from disarray to distinction, from slavery
to freedom. Centuries earlier, when the patriarch and his family entered Egypt, their reception was one of deference. But
pharaohs arose who knew not Joseph, and Jacob's posterity
fell to disrepute.

Now after 400 years of repression, deliverance was imminent. Nine of the plagues had already fallen, and the final
blight was winging earthward. Each family would experience
death to the firstborn. That is, unless the lamb had been appropriately sacrificed and eaten. There would be no excep-
tions, no exemptions, no second chances. The instructions
were clear, the stakes were high, the consequences were dire.

The lamb was their only hope of deliverance.

Our circumstances are similar. We too find ourselves enslaved in a land of wickedness, expecting a long-awaited freedom. And God is once again poised to bring deliverance. Everywhere the signs that are precursors of the end are being fulfilled. And final judgments are imminent. For us, as it was for them, the only hope of passing over into the freedom of our promised tomorrow is the faithful appropriation of the body and blood of the Lamb, Christ Jesus.

Notice how clearly the parallels between Israel's relationship to the typical and our relationship to the antitypical lamb arrange themselves. First to be observed, the *place* of the blood:

> Ye shall take a bunch of hyssop, and dip it in the blood that is in the bason, and strike the lintel and the two side posts with the blood that is in the bason; and none of you shall go out at the door of his house until the morning (Exodus 12:22).

The Passover experience focused on the primary unit of human endeavor—the individual home. The emphasis is unmistakable. There was to be a separate lamb for each house (see verse 3); they were to eat the Passover lamb in their own houses (see verse 7); there were to exclude all leaven for seven days from their houses (see verse 19); they were to wait with their children in their houses (see verse 22); they were to sprinkle the blood upon the portals and on the doorposts of their houses (see verse 22); no flesh was to be taken from their houses (see verse 46).

The lesson is clear. It is God's intention that our families—not our schools or our churches or any other institution in society—be the primary focus of salvation. The family is the fount of socialization, the place that gives primary character to the membership of the church. The inclination of this generation to make others responsible for establishing values is largely responsible for the spiritual decline of all institutions in our society. It is in the home where the principles of godliness should first be taught and where they should find their most insistent expression. That is the genius of God's instructions to Israel:

> These words, which I command thee this day, shall be in thine heart: and thou shalt teach them diligently unto thy children, and shalt talk of them when thou sittest in thine house, and when thou walkest by the way, and when thou liest down, and when thou risest up. And thou shalt bind them for a sign upon thine hand, and they shalt be as frontlets between thine eyes. And thou shalt write them upon the posts of thy house, and on thy gates (Deuteronomy 6:6-9).

Family devotions and private devotions—the two great boons of human spirituality—are, first of all, home events. No power on earth is as effective for the building of a virtuous citizenry. Our schools, our communities, our governments, our churches, are no more just, no more caring, no more effective, than the family units from which they are drawn. The Passover emphasizes God's design for the home as the primary place of character development and spiritual power.

The second lesson that is suggested by the Passover experience is the *prominence* of the blood: "They shall take of the blood, and strike it on the two side posts and on the upper door post of the houses, wherein they shall eat it" (Exodus 12:7).

There could be no mistakes. The blood was to be sprinkled on either side of the door and on the lintel above it. This stipulation directs that the blood be placed in the most visible of positions. Like a luminous garland draping the door frame, the sprinkled blood formed an arch over the entry of the worshipers' home. It was to be prominent, preeminent—the obvious focus for the occupants, for their neighbors, and especially for the sure, swift angel of death whom God would dispatch on that lethal mission.

And it is the same today. The blood of Christ should be the most visible component of our system of belief. Why? Because the sacrifice of Christ is the primary element of our salvation. All other doctrines or beliefs find meaning and importance in the blood. The Calvary event is the foundation element of Christian faith. As a fact in history, it proves the Father's love. As a sacrifice of Deity, it removes human guilt. As a narrative of love, it softens the human heart. As an acknowledged gift to humans, it awakens impulses to devotion and leads to surrender to the will of God. It is not the Sabbath or tithing or the prophetic dates and proof, which we so proudly hail, that convince, convict, and convert. It is the blood.

There is life in the blood. The nourishment of the brain and body is a function of the blood. Its properties contain the secrets of being. They hold the mysteries of human existence. Little wonder, then, that the blood of Jesus is the chief emblem of His salvation effort, and that the blood of animals was ordered shed as a foreshadowing of His death. He who ordained that the blood of lambs should be the sign of deliverance that Passover night long ago would have no less a priority for the blood of His Son today.

The third lesson that the Passover teaches us concerns the *procedures* of the blood. Each detail of the Passover process supplies rich instructions for our spiritual lives.

1. *The lamb was a male of the first year (verse 5).*

The age of the lamb symbolizes the youth of Christ at the time of His death. In Isaiah's words, "He was cut off out of the land of the living." His years were aborted, abruptly ended. His was not the privilege of threescore and ten. He did not die "full of years" but at the height of His strength, while His star was at its median.

2. *The lamb was without spot or blemish (verse 5).*

Tradition has it that the priestly inspection involved no less than fifty different inspection criteria. The regulations allowed no flaw of color, no twisted limbs, no cuts or bruises. Our true Lamb was that way. He was unsullied. He did no sin; neither was there any wickedness found in His mouth. He was holy and undefiled. He lived up to all the requirements of the law. With our human equipment, in the dreadful circumstances of a world degraded by 4,000 years of sin, He proved that Adam need not have sinned and that we who were born in sin can by His grace overcome our inherited and cultivated weaknesses.

3. *The lamb was slain at even (verse 6).*

It was at evening that the Saviour died. Matthew records that "when the even was come" (Matthew 27:57), His body was removed from the cross. As in the creation of the world, evening preceded morning; in the redemption of the world, the brightness of the resurrection was preceded by the dark shadows of Calvary.

4. *The lamb was eaten without leaven (verse 8).*

Leaven is a symbol of deceit, and the prohibition against its use during the Passover event is a perpetual warning against malice and hypocrisy among the waiting remnant.

5. *The lamb was to be eaten with bitter herbs (verse 8).*

The Passover meal was not a delightful feast, a banquet of pleasantries. It was eaten with bitter herbs, pungent reminders of the painful trials each believer experiences in the process of salvation: "All that will live godly . . . shall suffer persecution" (2 Timothy 3:12). Our salvation was not accomplished by pleasant acts. The Saviour suffered the painful wrath of demonic hatred, and so will we who claim His name.

6. *No bone in the lamb's body was to be broken (verse 46).*

Crucifixion was a slow, torturous death—usually requiring two or three days. A coroner of our time would probably give the primary cause of death as suffocation, resulting from the sagging of the upper body upon the chest, inhibiting the victim's ability to breathe. Sometimes to hasten death, the Romans broke the legs of the sufferer. But Jesus, who borrowed no divine assistance in His fight against sin, who drank no drugs to alleviate His pain, needed no assistance in dying. His human heart did not slowly suffocate from physical pressures. It was torn apart by the weight of our sins and the enormity of His mission.

7. *The lamb was not only slain, but eaten (v. 8).*

For Israel, the sacrifice was meaningless unless the flesh was consumed, internalized by the petitioner. For us, the death of Christ is ineffective unless we internalize Him by the daily study of His Word. He is the Word Incarnate, ingested, internalized, and assimilated. He is the secret of our daily growth, the Source of our overcoming.

8. *The uneaten portions of the lamb were burned and discarded (verse 10).*

No portion of the Passover lamb was left to decay. Neither did the body of our slain Lord suffer corruption. His molecular structure did not disintegrate. He was overcome by the pangs of death; but He did not experience the spoils of death; His body did not suffer putrefaction. Death overcame Him, but it could not undo Him.

9. *The lamb was to be eaten in haste (verse 11).*

The Israelites ate the lamb in haste, with staffs in hand, attired for travel. They awaited deliverance in expectant obedience, and so must we. Pilgrims in a land of plenty, strangers in our own global neighborhood, we trust the Lamb in glad anticipation of a final deliverance.

10. *The lamb was shared with those too poor to provide their own (verse 4).*

Israel's "lamb sharing" on the Passover night speaks to the mutuality of believers. Bearing one another's burdens and encouraging one another by word and deed, we are "our brothers' keepers." The church is mandated to carry the Good News to all of the world, but it is to one another that our first allegiance belongs.

11. *The lamb was shared with all non-Israelites who confessed the Passover God (verses 48, 49).*

God's decree that the paschal lamb be made available to believing Egyptians teaches us that the procedures and provisions of salvation are available to all. Christ is

Lord of all ethnicities, all languages, all classes.

The fourth and final truth to be observed focuses on the *power* of the blood. The Passover drama unfolded with ever-increasing intensity. The children were gathered from neighboring homes and fields of play. The father, cradling the furry, unsuspecting lamb in his arms, plunged the jagged knife in the neck of the animal and drew it across the pulsating jugular vein, creating an instant stream of rich, red blood. The dying lamb contorted in pain, then, limp from loss of blood, closed its eyes in death. The stream of blood mixed with the briny tears of the sorrowful suppliant and collected thickly in the basin below.

Then the father dipped the hyssop branch into the warm blood and sprinkled it above and on either side of the door. The carcass was prepared for roasting. Parents and children gathered at the family table to eat the meal and to await their fate. Would their firstborn be spared? Had they forgotten some detail that would invalidate their preparation? Would the God who reads hearts and motives see in their efforts some strain of guilt or insincerity? In spite of the sign of the blood, would He afflict their home with the curse of death? In awe, the families watched and prayed, huddled in tearful expectation, each heart throbbing with fearful dread. And then it happened—the death angel struck. The Scripture reads:

It came to pass, that at midnight the Lord smote all the firstborn in the land of Egypt, from the firstborn of Pharaoh that sat on his throne unto the firstborn of the captive that was in the dungeon; and all the firstborn of cattle. . . . And there was a great cry in Egypt; for there was not a house where there was not one dead (Exodus 12:29, 30).

But while devastation befell the Egyptians, the avenger "passed over" all the houses in which God's instructions had been faithfully followed. Such is the power of the blood. It saves absolutely, but it condemns with finality. The fate of the households of Egypt is but a weak representation of the final outpouring of the wrath of God. The divine Watcher, whose Spirit will not always strive with humanity, "has appointed a day in which to judge the world in righteousness." The sinfulness of selfish, intemperate, profane, secular humanity will not go unrewarded. The fires reserved for the devil and his angels will also consume those who join the rebellious resistance.

By the power of the blood, God is now free to exact justice without sacrificing mercy. That was not possible before Calvary. There, mercy's hands were nailed that justice's hands might be freed. Now God can destroy without denying mercy. So complete will be the destruction of the wicked that there will be left of them, neither "root nor branch" (Malachi 4:1).

But God can now also forgive without compromising justice. And, this—the salvation of the righteous—is an even greater testimony to the power of the blood than is the destruction of the wicked. The righteous are saved, not because they have acquired traits that make them fit for heaven, but because the blood of Jesus has paid the debt for their sins and His righteous robe substitutes for their yet-undone condition. How wondrous! Blood, valuable enough to pay our debt; powerful enough to eradicate our sins; royal enough to effect our adoption; righteous enough to stay our recompense, to bring beauty for ashes, riches for rags, life for death, infinity for finitude, transcendence for transitoriness, eternal deliverance for the shame and pain of everlasting loss.

Peace is very rare in any of today's communities. Nevertheless, it is an absolute requirement for Christian living. According to Paul, peace comes from the heart of God and is transmitted by principles that must be understood by all those who desire to do His will.

Chapter 10

Above All, Faith

"Above all, taking the shield of faith, wherewith ye shall be able to quench all the fiery darts of the wicked" (Ephesians 6:16).

Faith, Webster states, is firm belief in something for which there is no proof. In other words, when a fact or theory is proven, faith is not required. Faith operates only where proof is not present. Faith and proof are coterminous; they are mutually exclusive! Faith is trusting what you cannot prove, believing what you cannot understand, following where you cannot see, depending upon what you do not have. It is "perceiving as real fact what is not revealed to the senses" (Hebrews 11:1, Amplified Bible).

And, not too surprisingly, faith is a rare commodity in our day. It is not compatible with the burgeoning sensuality of our acquisitive generation. Ours is an age of faithless unbelief, a society of profane, sensate, mundane concerns. Our Lord foresaw that scarcity and asked in rhetorical condemnation, "When the Son of man cometh, shall he find faith on the earth?" (Luke 18:8). And, yet, since "the just shall live by faith" and since in the final analysis "faith is the victory," it remains a categorical absolute, an unalterable must, the part of our Christian armor to be extended above all others.

Faith has a number of characteristics that go against the grain of contemporary lifestyle. One is *waiting*. We moderns don't like to wait. We are a people of the proverbial pell-mell mentality, or better stated, the "instant" syndrome. We have instant travel, instant communication, instant food, instant credit, instant cash, and, alas, even instant love, instant marriage, and instant divorce. We *do not* like to wait. We press buttons, pull levers, push handles, turn dials, flip switches, punch numbers, and we get what we want. We don't like to wait. We have computers, fax machines, microwave ovens, sidewalk tellers, car telephones, one-hour laundry service, two-minute carwashes, and, in the city where I live, pizza delivered within thirty minutes anywhere in town. Our predecessors had to wait, but we are self-sufficient, selfcontained, and self-fulfilled. Waiting and depending upon forces we cannot control is contrary to our way.

And then faith involves *abstractness*—the ability to reason about God without factual contact with His being. Such effort is difficult for our society. Proof is what our generation requires. We depend upon tangible hardware, critical demonstration, empirical evidence; we glory in the scientific method. Our procedures require test-tube sureness, quantifiable verification. We believe what we see, what we can establish with graphs and charts and sure percentages. We are manipulators of the concrete reality about us, distinctly disinclined to dependence upon abstract factors.

Faith also involves *trusting*, another difficult virtue for our times. And good reason exists for the moral skepticism of our society. We are daily bombarded with news of rampant embezzlement and deception, bribe-taking judges, dope-dealing policemen, and philandering clergymen. We live with the reality of fraudulent contracts and broken promises, of institutional hypocrisy and of government scandals that fulfill the biblical description of "spiritual wickedness in high places." Ethics is not in vogue. Most of our pledges do bind "as ropes of sand," too many of our heroes have feet of clay, and it is easy to believe that everybody is doing it. We have become an impatient, cynical, skeptical society. We are, as Ellen White predicted, a generation "almost destitute of . . . faith" (*Spiritual Gifts*, vol. 3, p. 94). And that is tragic, for Scripture makes it clear that we must "follow after . . . faith" (1 Timothy 6:11), that we must "fight the good fight of faith" (1 Timothy 6:12), that "we walk by faith, and not by sight" (2 Corinthians 5:7), that "without faith it is impossible to please him" (Hebrews 11:6)

Why is faith so essential to our spiritual success? First and foremost, it is our only way of knowing God. When Paul stated, "Eye hath not seen, nor ear heard, neither have entered into the heart of man, the things which God hath prepared for them that love him," he intended not so much a heavenly "grab bag" awaiting the redeemed, but he was reminding us of the inability of human sense to interpret celestial matter. First Corinthians 2:9 is God's reminder that the appointments of heaven are beyond our comprehension, that Christianity is a leap from the sure ground of absolute verification onto the high platform of absolute trust. Faith is our only way of relating to God. It is not only impossible to please Him without faith. It is impossible to know Him.

The second reason that faith is such a critical part of our spiritual armament is that it is the ultimate defense against Satan's discouragements. Among the deadliest of weapons of ancient warriors were arrows dipped in fire. The King James Version of Ephesians 6:16 calls these "fiery darts"; the Living Bible calls these missiles "fiery arrows"; the Good News Bible sees them as "burning arrows"; the Amplified Bible has them as "flaming missiles." But in any translation or language, the meaning is the same: we are in a life-and-death struggle with Satan, and it is the shield of faith more than any other spiritual armament that keeps us from being jarred and scarred by his lethal devices. Because the shields of the ancients were soaked in solutions that extinguished the arrows' flames, they represent well the function of faith and remind us that, saturated with obedient trust, faith is our primary protection from spiritual chaos.

Every child of God is a prime target for Satan's missiles. Our allegiance to Christ guarantees confrontation and struggle. The enemy targets us with the bullets of fanaticism, the arrows of pleasure, the gases of prosperity, the torches of racial injustice, the darts of gender discrimination, the painful artillery of character assassination, the crippling flak of physical affliction, and the maiming shells of ambitions deferred and hoped denied.

There are times when only faith will do, when reason is not enough, when the clouds obscure God's smiling face and we must trust Him where we cannot trace Him. There are times when there are no answers, when things just don't add up, when life isn't fair, when love is unrequited and motives misunderstood, when hopes are dashed by unalterable circumstances and logic does not prevail. That is why Paul warned every would-be soldier: "Strap on the girdle of truth, buckle up the breastplate of righteousness, pull down the helmet of salvation, pick up the sword of the Spirit, tie on the coverings of peace." In other words, "Put on the whole armor," but hold above all the shield of faith.

From where does faith emanate? First and foremost from the Word of God. "So then faith cometh by hearing, and hearing by the word of God" (Romans 10:17). Faith in God is generated in the human breast by the dynamics of Scripture. The Word of God holds life-giving energies, which bring into existence the spiritual manifestations of faith. The Bible is the soil in which faith germinates, finds root, and then flowers into a fruit-bearing activity. That process cannot be logically diagrammed or completely understood. Neither can it be duplicated in any other source. However, this much we do know: crassly materialistic, intemperate, faithless, profligate humans who read the Book with a desire to know God gradually come to see things differently. They don't just see old reality in a new light, but begin to see new reality in the world about them.

And faith also comes by observation. While it is true that faith is not demonstration, it is not without its referrals. Ellen White helps us by stating, "The doubt that demands perfect knowledge will never yield to faith. Faith rests upon evidence, not demonstration" (*Selected Messages,* bk. 1, p. 28). What evidence?

1. The evidence of *nature.* That was David's testimony. When overwhelmed by the majesty, the beauty, the regularity, and the immensity of the stellar skies, he cried: "The heavens declare the glory of God, and the firmament showeth his handiwork" (Psalm 19:1, 2).

2. The testimony of *our daily experience.* The long list of prayers answered, problems solved, miracles witnessed establishes faith. Faith, in essence, is not so much confidence in a proposition as confidence in the proposer, not so much trust in a theory as in the theoretician, not belief in a promise but in the promisor. We Christians not only believe *about* Christ, we believe *in* Him.

Each blessing establishes our trust, each victory strengthens our confidence, until the chain of faith forged in the furnace of trial and deliverance becomes an invincible link with God. And we learn to trust Him, not only when times are good and blessings are evident. On a deeper level, we trust Him when we suffer and when we do not understand. This is the "Thy will be done" commitment of those rare disciples who do not love God because He removes the mountains of trial and valleys of suffering, but because He provides the strength for climbing and grace of endurance. Such faith that permits us, like the Hebrews, to stand before the furnace of affliction and cry, "Our God is able to deliver us. But if not, we will not bow down," and to say with Job, "Though He slay me, yet will I trust Him." It is such genuine, absolute confidence that the apostle had in mind when he said, "Above all—faith!"

And there is one more means of faith growth that deserves our attention. That is *our individual testimony* to the goodness of God. Revelation 12:11 informs us that the redeemed shall overcome "by the blood of the Lamb, and by the word of their testimony." We are not only strengthened by what God has done for us. We are blessed anew when we tell others of His dealings on our behalf. "It is a good thing to give thanks unto the Lord" (Psalm 92:1). Nothing so stifles spiritual growth as discouragement. Those Christians who dwell on the distaff side of life, whose dominant strains are the blue notes of disappointment, whose eyes are trained upon the seamy sights of human treachery and faltering faith, soon lose faith.

God's book of remembrance, as Malachi reminds us, is for those who love the Lord and speak often of His name (see Malachi 3:16). That is what Ellen White meant when she said, "Let us not talk doubt, but faith. . . . If we lay hold upon this power, and do not trust in our own human strength, we shall see the salvation of God" (*Selected Messages*, bk. 1, p. 85). Negativism toward the church, toward our fellow human beings, toward our individual experience is not possible when we remember the goodness of the Lord. It is true that even the saints must "walk through the valley of the shadow of death," but it is also true that He "restoreth" our souls. As we witness to each other of God's love and compassion, recounting for one another incidents of divine care and personal victories, our faith is strengthened.

Genuine faith in God flavors the entire psyche. It produces a buoyancy about life, it stiffens our determination, emboldens our resolve, and ennobles our fellowship. It allows us to be courageous without being egotistical, determined without being dogmatic, disappointed without being discouraged, delayed without being downhearted, down without being out. We are sometimes in disarray, but never in despair. Why is this possible? One reason is that genuine faith eradicates anxieties about what others think of us or say about us and fastens our concern upon the approbation of God. Then we can sing with David:

The Lord is my light and my salvation; whom shall I fear? the Lord is the strength of my life; of whom shall I be afraid? When the wicked, even mine enemies and my foes, came upon me to eat up my flesh, they stumbled and fell. Though an host should encamp against me, my heart shall not fear: though war should rise against me, in this will I be confident (Psalm 27:1-3).

And faith increases our productivity, our capacity for effectiveness. That is exactly what Jesus meant when He said, "According to your faith be it unto you" (Matthew 9:29). Faith is a variable in God's requirements for reward, and the more of it we have, the more of His blessings He bestows. Faith is not idle dependence. It is, rather, the "fighting in the valley while expecting help from the hills" kind of activity that David advised (see Psalm 121:1). It is the going as far as you can, doing the best that you can, "giving it all that you have" kind of effort that the Hebrews manifested. Their example confirms that "it is the very essence of all right faith to do the right thing at the right time" (*Testimonies*, vol. 6, p. 24).

Faith is praying for food and setting the table; it is praying for rain and putting your boots on; it is praying for tuition and registering your children; faith is sharing trust with the mother of Christ, who confidently advised the wedding host, "Whatsoever he saith . . . do it" (John 2:5).

One of my favorite poems reads:

Said the robin to the sparrow, "I should really like
to know
Why these anxious human beings rush about and worry
so."
Said the sparrow to the robin, "Friend, I think that it
must be
That they have no heavenly Father such as cares for you
and me."

Presumption attempts results while ignoring the prerequisites of success. But faith approaches consequences secure in its ongoing relationship with Christ, resolutely believing that "no good thing will he withhold from them that walk uprightly." It accepts that when we have done our part, the consequences are always for our best good. Faith is an enabling confidence that frees us to attempt exploits in God's name. Faith is not only a measure of our love for God, it is a basis of His response to our needs, an index to our usefulness. No wonder Paul challenged us: "Above all, faith."

And there is more. In addition to relieving our anxieties and increasing our productivity, genuine faith adds to our longevity:

The relation that exists between the mind and the body is very intimate. When one is affected, the other sympathizes. The condition of the mind affects the health to a far greater degree than many realize. Many of the diseases from which men suffer are the result of mental depression. Grief, anxiety, discontent, remorse, guilt, distrust, all tend to break down the life forces and to invite decay and death (*The Ministry of Healing*, p. 241).

This is what Solomon meant when he said, "A merry heart doeth good like a medicine" (Proverbs 17:22). Mirth and revelry last but for a moment, but Christian joy is a way of life, a mind-set, an attitude rooted in an abiding trust in a caring God. Such a faith purges the mind of despair, purifies the mind of bitterness, polices the mind of envy and greed, and, since the state of mind influences the state of body, sets into motion dynamics that vitalize the system, aiding in bodily health. Faith is not just a psychological principle, it is a physiological force. It stimulates us to commandment keeping, which adds "length of days, and long life, and peace" (Proverbs 3:2). It generates the pleasant words, which are "sweet to the soul, and health to the bones" (Proverbs 16:24). It produces the calm spirit, which is life to the body (see Proverbs 14:30, Amplified Bible).

And the converse is also true. If being cheerful benefits health, "a broken spirit dries the bones" (Proverbs 17:22, Amplified Bible). Whereas faith breeds the cheerful mind that stimulates health, faithlessness results in a pessimism of spirit that depresses the nerves and tends toward disease. Those whose thoughts are prone to stay "where doubts arise and fears dismay" eventually experience the physical ills characterized in Scripture as a "rottenness of the bones" (Proverbs 14:30). No wonder Paul admonishes that whereas all our spiritual armament is vital, we must over all brandish faith.

Faith is the taproot of our spiritual development. It is our anchor of peace in the turbulent tides of life. It is the golden chord that binds us together and ties us to the heart of God, and so it has ever been to the followers of the Lord. By faith Abel offered, by faith Enoch walked, by faith Noah built, by faith Abraham obeyed, by faith Jacob wrestled, by faith Moses chose, by faith Job endured, by faith Elijah prayed, by faith Nehemiah built, by faith Job suffered, by faith Esther committed, by faith the paralytic walked, by faith the centurion sought, by faith the Baptist dared, by faith Philip shared. Faith was, in fact, a determinative factor in the sacrifice of our Lord. His entire ministry was a life of trust, that is, faith in the Father. He did not function here as God. He took on human garb and lived by the rules of human nature, trusting in the Father's will and power, solemnly declaring, "I can of mine own self do nothing" (John 5:30).

In the wilderness alone, living without the benefit of earthly comforts, fleeing the angry mobs, or suffering from the desertion of the Twelve, our Lord was stabilized by His faith in the promises of the Father. There is never a hint of wavering or doubt in His experience until in Gethsemane and at Calvary, where His faith underwent its deepest trial. Here our champion of righteousness, who had won every battle, from the confirmation by John to the condemnation by Pilate, staggered beneath the enormity of His role. Hanging there as our Substitute, suffering God's wrath upon sin and sinners,

> the Saviour could not see through the portals of the tomb. Hope did not present to Him His coming forth from the grave a conqueror, or tell Him of the Father's acceptance of the sacrifice. He feared that sin was so offensive to God that Their separation was to be eternal (*The Desire of Ages*, p. 753).

Amid the darkness that enveloped the cross, the most crucial of decisions was made. The struggle in which He engaged there was indeed the fight of faith. In those dreadful hours, the faith of Christ sagged heavily. Racked with pain, ravaged with fears, and ridden with the guilt and loneliness of all deserving sinners, Jesus' humanity withdrew from the horrors of crucifixion. But it was here, at the vortex of redemption's plan, that faith's grandest victory was won. Recalling the evidence of His Father's love, which He had known during His earthly sojourn, a surge of confidence swept through His being. In absolute faith in His Father's will, He pierced the darkness that engulfed Him with His dying but triumphant cry: "Father, into thy hands I commend my spirit" (Luke 23:46).

Someday, when we shall cast our crowns at His pierced feet and gaze upon His thorn-scarred brow, when we shall kneel beneath His nail-pierced hands, there to be known even as we are known, faith will no longer be necessary. Its ministry will be completed; all will be visible. But until then, we soldiers of the cross must fight on in full armor, always trusting the providence of God, always exalting the shield of faith.

The church is no ordinary institution. It is established of God and functions by rules that He has ordained. Its history and role are sacred, its charter and authority are divine. Paul knew that and gave the Thessalonians and all other congregations under his care clear evidence of this view.

Chapter 11

I Am Not Ashamed

"For I am not ashamed of the gospel of Christ: for it is the power of God unto salvation to every one that believeth; to the Jew first, and also to the Greek" *(Romans 1:16).*

Without a doubt, the book of Romans is Paul's most systematic presentation of the gospel. In it we find his clarion treatment of the relation between faith and works. We also find his sharpest contrast of the "justification which is a gift" and that which is wrought by the believer. His statements regarding the essentials of faith in this epistle bring joyful excitement to the sincere reader and are unsurpassed in imagery and impact. But our text is not found in the deeper theological treatises of Romans; it comes at the conclusion of his typically warm and vibrant introduction. Here he summarizes his pride of fellowship and his joy in apostleship by saying, "I am not ashamed of the gospel of Christ." And neither should we be! We should not be ashamed of the gospel nor of the church that God has established for its study and dissemination, the body of believers who trust His Word and perpetuate His message.

And it is true. I am not ashamed of the *origins of the*

96

church. The promise to John regarding God's people of the last days is: "There appeared a great wonder in heaven; a woman clothed with the sun, and the moon under her feet, and upon her head a crown of twelve stars."

"And the dragon was wroth with the woman, and went to make war with the remnant of her seed, which keep the commandments of God, and have the testimony of Jesus Christ" (Revelation 12:1, 17).

In prophetic understanding, the woman represents the church, the dragon is the devil, and remnant means an "end-time" people. Seen thusly, these verses provide a series of significant indicators concerning our subject group. They prophecy of a people who anticipate the coming of Christ: (a) clothed in the sun, that is, possessing the complete system of gospel truth; (b) having the moon under their feet, that is, enjoying a working knowledge of the highly illustrative systems of Moses; (c) wearing a crown of twelve stars, that is, demonstrating the faith and zeal of the twelve apostles; (d) keeping the commandments of God, that is, obeying the ten words of the moral law; and (e) having the testimony of Jesus, that is, receiving and obeying the voice of prophetic guidance.

Does society record the rise of such a group in these remnant times? Yes. In fact, as early as the 1820s a Scottish prelate named Edward Irving was inspired to preach in the British Isles the good news of the second coming of Christ. About the same time, Joseph Wolff launched upon a distinguished career that eventually took him to Asia, Asia Minor, Africa, Europe, and the United States, preaching the advent and emphasizing the first of the three angels' messages.

Meanwhile, on the eastern shore of the United States, a godly farmer named William Miller was also inspired with these themes. Impressed of the Holy Spirit that the end was near and that final judgment had come, Miller established cottage meetings and study groups throughout New England for investigation of this exciting event. Johann Bengel in Germany, Louis Gaussen in Switzerland, and Manuel Lacunza in South America preached these stimulating prophecies to their hearers. In Holland, a royal museum keeper by the name of

Henry Heintzpeter saw it in a dream and joined the others in preaching. In Sweden, where the state prohibited worship not conducted in state churches by official clergymen, little children, unlearned in letters but initiated in the prophecies by the Holy Spirit, preached at gatherings in private homes. Their simple but moving faith impacted hundreds with the news of the judgment as found in the prophecies of Daniel and Revelation.

God had told Daniel earlier, "But thou, O Daniel, shut up the words, and seal up the book, even to the time of the end." Now just when Henry Ford would put the world on wheels and the Wright brothers would give humans wings, just when conditions were developing that would indeed send many "running to and fro," understanding in the book of Daniel was also given to God's chosen but scattered servants around the world.

This spiritual awakening was not of human devising. It was not the studied plan of calculating religious entrepreneurs. This was the spontaneous combustion of spiritual energies turned loose by heaven in fulfillment of events earlier predicted. It was the woman, stepping out of the shadows; it was Elijah, walking again upon the highways of earth. It was the three angels, proclaiming their stirring message to this world's final inhabitants. The time had come. God pulled down the handle on the switch box of prophecy, and the lights of truth went on around the globe. As might be expected, with time, those who had been similarly illumined concerning the judgment were drawn toward each other, coalescing into what were at first loose associations but what later became a formally organized church.

A number of events critical to the development of the church's superstructure stand out as milestones in this process: The baptism of Ellen White in 1842; the Port Gibson Conference on Consolidation in 1845; the six Sabbath conferences in 1848; the printing of *The Present Truth* by James White in 1848; the first church building in 1849; the first ministerial credentials issued in 1850; the first deacons chosen in 1851; the first printing press erected in 1852; the first church school in 1853; the beginnings of the literature ministry in 1854; the beginnings of annual state meetings (now called camp meetings) in 1859; the installation of the tithing system in 1859; the adoption of the name Seventh-day Adventists in 1860; the first conference organization of 1861; the election of the first General Conference president (John Byington) and Ellen White's first comprehensive "health" vision in 1863. The rest is a grand and glorious history of battles fought through decades of wars and famines and droughts and persecutions on every continent and in almost every country of the world. It is a thrilling story as gripping as it is telling— and I am not ashamed.

And, I am not ashamed of the *name* of this church—Seventh-day Adventist. Now, there are a lot of other names. I was approached on a busy street in New York City several years ago by a young man who thrust out his hand and said, "Hello, brother. Are you sanctified?" I knew immediately what he meant. He wanted to know whether or not I am a member of the Sanctified Church. If I had said No, I would have risked a lecture regarding the virtues of the name *sanctified*. If I had said Yes, I would have risked having to answer questions relative to the Sanctified congregation I attended. I considered the risks and said, "Yes, I am sanctified." He didn't question me further, but if he had, I was ready. He didn't know it, but what I meant was that since I serve a God who is sanctified, since I'm striving to live a life that is sanctified, since I worship on the day that He blessed and hallowed and sanctified, and since I belong to a church that is being sanctified by Christ's blood, I feel free to claim Sanctification.

And then there is the name Baptist. This name advertises that church's affirmation of baptism by immersion in contrast to pouring or sprinkling. I believe in immersion also. That's the way Jesus did it and the way we all should. My church is strong on immersion, so with that distinction in view, I am Baptist also.

And then there is the name Catholic. Catholicity means universality, a prominent characteristic of the church in which I have membership. With companies and congregations housing over six million members in 184 countries of the world, we are catholic in the best sense of the word. In the true light of these names, I am not only Sanctified and Baptist, but Catholic, as well.

Others say, "I belong to the Church of the Latter-day Saints." Do I have a text for that! In fact, in clinching his portrait of the remnant who would fulfill the three angels' mission, John wrote, "Here is the patience of the saints: here are they that keep the commandments of God." Similar analysis can be drawn with almost every name. The Church of God, the Church of God in Christ, the Nazarenes, the Pentecostals, the Methodists, the Jehovah's Witnesses, etc. All of these names are good, as far as they go. They just don't go far enough. The name Seventh-day Adventist assumes the primary virtues that each advertises and adds the two major tenets that they have failed to emphasize, the seventh-day Sabbath and the second coming of Christ. Thus we can agree that:

> The name Seventh-day Adventist carries the true features of our faith in front and will convict the inquiring mind. Like an arrow from the Lord's quiver, it will wound the transgressors of God's law, and will lead to repentance toward God and faith in our Lord Jesus Christ (*Testimonies for the Church* , vol. 1, p. 224).

And I am not ashamed of the *doctrines* of our church. I'm happy about the doctrine of health reform. What an advantage to know that the proper use of fresh air, water, food, exercise, sunshine, rest, work, along with trust in God, enhances the quality of life and maximizes one's longevity. I'm especially glad that I was taught while a little boy that my stomach is not a graveyard, that when an animal dies, it is not to be masticated or internalized, that is, buried and then assimilated within my body.

I'm happy for the doctrine of dress reform, that I need not become agitated about every style that comes from Paris or Hollywood or Montreal or from wherever they emanate. And may I share a secret with you? Hold on to whatever the style is that you have now. Put it away, but save it. I promise you that if time lasts long enough, it will be in vogue again. Narrow ties give way to wide ties. When wide ties go out of style, the narrow ones come back again. The fashion parade is a slavish cycle. Frugal Christians can look good without being duped by the designers and mercenary accomplices, whose wild imaginations and material greed bind multitudes in blind, unhealthy conformity.

And I'm glad that I know the state of the dead. I don't have to be afraid of spirits and spooks and ghosts. I found out a long time ago that it's not the dead who are making the trouble. The noises I hear in the dark, the figures and voices some people identify at séances, are not the dead but the enemy who causes death. And when I call on the name of Jesus, Satan unfailingly retreats. The blessed hope of the resurrection frees me from cynicism about life, and the blessed knowledge of One mightier than our wily foe frees me from superstition and fear regarding death.

I'm particularly happy about the doctrine of the Sabbath. In fact, the older I get, the more I understand the need and benefits of Sabbath rest. Yes, the Sabbath is for worship and the Sabbath is for service, but it is especially, God said, a day of rest. If your Sabbath begins with a last-minute dash to be at church on time and continues with your counting money during Sabbath School or church service, passing out tracts all afternoon, visiting the old folks' home in the evening, teacher's meeting at night, and church board after that, you don't really know what Sabbath keeping is all about. The Sabbath was made for man and not man for the Sabbath. And while true Sabbath observance includes fellowship and sharing and witness, it should provide soul-refreshing, body-relaxing, nerve-calming rest and restoration. It is a happy part of our doctrinal heritage.

And all of our doctrines are like that: tithing, conversion, the second coming. They are all Bible-based fundamentals that enhance our numbers, guard our borders, nurture our souls, prepare us for a richer life in a better world.

And I am not ashamed of the *organization* of this church: the General Conference, the division conferences, the union conferences, the local conferences and missions, the individual church, the auxiliaries in the church, and the members of the church.

Now it is true that sometimes there are problems on board the old ship of Zion. There are times when leaders, as well as members, err in virtue and in judgment. Some people have become discouraged because their hopes for a perfect church have not been met. Too bad! Christians who know that one-third of the heavenly host were expelled for rebellion should not be surprised to find apostasy among God's people on earth. Perhaps we would all do well to remember Dwight L. Moody's words to the youth who told him he wouldn't join any church until he found the one that was absolutely perfect. "If you do find such a group," Moody replied, "please don't join it because it won't be perfect anymore."

The burning question, however, is *why*? With such assurance and knowledge, why is the church still "wilderness wandering"? Why are we yet in the desert of society, looking and longing for the Promised Land? When the harvest is so ripe, why is our reaping so small? Why haven't our results matched our expectations? There is no doubt about it. In name, in doctrine, in organization, in mission, and history, we are accurate, we are confirmed, we are sure of our roots and clear in our mission. Why, then, the delay?

Why? Because we have fulfilled all the indicators except one, and that one is the challenge given to Laodicea, the final segment of church history: "To him that overcometh will I grant to sit with me in my throne, even as I also overcame, and am sat down with my Father in his throne" (Revelation 3:21). And what must we overcome before we can experience victory? Our pride, our materialism, our selfishness, our lethargy, our evil speaking, our evil listening, and our dependence upon our own works instead of the righteousness of Christ.

My favorite illustration of this need is provided in the case of the missionary who, after a lengthy service with a tribe of

Indians in the Peruvian Andes, retired to his home and family many thousands of miles away. His farewell service was filled with grateful expressions and deep regrets. His had been a long and joyous stay among his adopted people. There was one happy note to this goodbye. He promised that he would send a replacement, a younger, more vigorous man who would soon come to continue the ministry of teaching and healing that he had established. As the pastor turned to leave, the chief called, "But, wait, how will we know him?" The pastor described various characteristics that would identify his replacement, but the wise old chief would take no chances. In full view of his people, he broke in half a small, smooth stone and gave the departing missionary one piece, while keeping the other. "Tell your friend to bring this half when he comes," the chief said. "That way we can be sure."

A few months later, the people watched with excitement as a party of white men arrived at their settlement. A handsome young man greeted the chief, and asked to meet the entire tribe in prayer and discussion. "That's fine," the chief said, "but where is your stone?" Baffled by the question, the young missionary confessed that he had his Bible, his picture scroll, his charts and graphs, his songbooks, but no stone. "You, then, are not the right man," the chief replied. "Thank you for coming, but you need not stay. We're looking for the man with the stone."

Back with his party the youth reported his odd experience. "The people are nice; they seem receptive to the gospel, but they are very superstitious. They demanded that I carry stones." The decision was made. They would send someone else with stones. Some time later, another young man arrived with pockets full of stones. "Why have you come?" asked the chief. "To preach and teach," replied the visitor. "But do you have the stone?" the old chief inquired. "Oh, yes," the young missionary answered, and with a smile and with great confidence he produced a handful of stones of various shapes and sizes. "You have stones," the chief said, "but not the right stone."

Much later, another party of white men arrived, and

another smiling young preacher made his intentions known. When he had given his name and stated his purpose, he was asked, "Where is the stone?" Reaching into his pocket, he pulled out the half that his predecessor had given him. The excited chief produced the half he had so closely guarded. The thrill of that moment was but the beginning of another long and productive service for the cause of truth.

Christ our Redeemer, our Rock, the Foundation and Cornerstone of the church, is Himself the match to the Old Testament prophecies of a coming Messiah. His birth in the lineage of Judah was predicted in Genesis 49:10 and fulfilled in Luke 3:23. His coming in the city of Bethlehem was predicted in Micah 5:2 and fulfilled in Matthew 2:1. His conception by a virgin was predicted in Isaiah 7:14 and fulfilled in Matthew 1:18. His flight into Egypt was predicted in Hosea 11:1 and fulfilled in Matthew 2:14. His ministry among the poor was predicted in Isaiah 61:1 and fulfilled in Luke 4:18, 19. His entry into Jerusalem were predicted in Zechariah 9:9 and fulfilled in John 12:13. His selling price of thirty pieces of silver was predicted in Zechariah 11:12 and fulfilled in Matthew 26:15. His humiliation and suffering were predicted in Isaiah 53 and fulfilled in John 19:33. His burial was predicted in Isaiah 53:9 and fulfilled in John 19:38-42. His resurrection was predicted in Psalm 16:10 and fulfilled in Mark 16:9. His ascension was predicted in Psalm 68:18 and fulfilled in Luke 24:51.

There is no doubt about it. We hold up the Old Testament in one hand and the life and love of Jesus in the other. It is a perfect match, an absolute fit. He is not just "historical Jesus." He is *actual Lord*, He is God Incarnate. He is our unmistakable unity of expectation and reality. So it is to be with us who claim the promise of the Elijah people, the woman dressed in the sun, and the three angels who cry over planet Earth. The symbolisms in these models cry for total fulfillment in our daily lives.

And what will make that happen? I point you to the Scriptures. It is by the searching, quickening rays of the Word of God that we are made, not simply students of prophecy, but exhibits of salvation—not simply knowledgeable religionists but a corporate colony of committed disciples. We are not just another Christian fellowship, but a people of destiny, ever grateful, ever humble, and *never* ashamed.

As 1 Thessalonians, chapter 1, details, Paul was not shy about his personal testimony. How did he go about his growth experience? What were the dynamics of his character development? Fortunately for us, he was willing to speak of his growth in grace in many of his letters.

Chapter 12

On Your Marks, Get Set, Go!

"Brethren, I count not myself to have apprehended; but this one thing I do, forgetting those things which are behind, and reaching forth unto those things which are before, I press toward the mark for the prize of the high calling of God in Christ Jesus" (Philippians 3:13, 14).

Philippians is often described as a "thank-you note," in which Paul also reminds the church of its need to model after Christ in humility and other essential Christian virtues. That, of itself, does not distinguish this letter greatly from his other epistles. What does is his unique description in chapter three—the *how* of Christian success. He does so by drawing lessons from the races of his day, which included the Olympic events of which the Romans were so very fond.

In fact, Paul references athletic activities in several of his epistles. He reasoned with the Ephesians regarding wrestling with the enemy (see Ephesians 6:12); he spoke to the Corinthians regarding boxing or fighting for the victor's crown (see 1 Corinthians 9:25, 26); and in a number of places he used the analogy of the runner to drive home important counsel. His advice is that Christians run with purpose (see 1 Corinthians 9:24), with dedication (see 1 Corinthians 9:25), with persistence (see Galatians 5:7), with effectiveness (see Philippians 2:16), with patience (see Hebrews, 12:1), and without incumbrance (see Hebrews 12:1). But it is in Philippians 3:13, 14 that the apostle provides his most picturesque application of the runner's challenge.

The lessons are accurate and impressive. He begins by confessing, "Brethren, I count not myself to have apprehended" (Philippians 3:13). This statement conforms precisely to the first of the three commands given all sprinters as they prepare to compete. The starter's hand is raised, and the cry is given: "On your marks!" At this order, the runners assume their positions, crouching low in their designated lanes. The moment of truth has arrived. All for which they have sacrificed and trained is now about to happen. In ordinary races the victory means personal satisfaction and material reward. In the major events, such as the world-class competition of Paul's society and ours, victory means national pride, and loss, national shame and embarrassment. Wise runners go down "on the marks" hopeful but not boastful, always knowing that victory is a reality only when the finish line is crossed. It is that attitude of humility and self-abnegation that the king of Israel referenced when he said to Ben-Hadad, king of Syria, "Let not him that girdeth on his harness boast himself as he that putteth it off" (1 Kings 20:11), and that which Paul conveys when he confesses, "I have not yet attained."

Basic to his attitude is Paul's increasingly clear view of the righteousness of Christ. The more he understood of the holiness of Christ, the more he breathed the atmosphere of Calvary, the less he thought of his own goodness. So overwhelmed was he by the vision of Christ's righteousness that he described himself a wretched man (see Romans 7:24) and a chief of sinners (see 1 Timothy 1:15), and he is not alone in such an assessment. Isaiah, who saw the high and holy God, cried, "O wretched man that I am," and the six-winged seraphims themselves, when they come into God's presence, with two wings fly, with two wings cover their feet, and with two wings hide their faces.

Paul's humility was more than the demurring manifested by Moses and Gideon, who, overwhelmed by the call to duty, sought reassurance for their tasks. Neither was his the lament of an aging professional, expressing remorse regarding a fading career with goals undone. His was a far deeper realization—the knowledge of spiritual inadequacy and the need for the infusions of grace and righteousness to fuel and sustain his energies.

Having expressed that need, Paul then characterizes the second of the starter's commands by stating, "This one thing I do" (Philippians 3:13). The first command is "On your marks!" The second is "Get set!" Now the runners plant their feet firmly against the starting blocks and raise themselves from their knees, leaning forward in excited anticipation of the final command, the signal to begin. At the command "Get set," runners become physically and psychologically geared for the task ahead. Nothing else matters. All other thoughts are cast aside. The race is all that counts. For Paul, this focus is achieved when he mates his attitude of humility with the single-minded determination that drives him to readiness and brooks no other priority.

Single-minded dedication to the requisites of holiness is a prime demand of salvation. That is what Christ meant when He said, "No man can serve two masters: for either he will hate the one, and love the other; or else he will hold to the one and despise the other" (Matthew 6:24). It is what He also meant when He taught from the mount that it would better to pluck out the eye or cut off the hand that offends and go into heaven maimed but totally focused, than to enter hellfire with divided loyalties. Further, it is what Paul had in mind when he asks, "Who shall separate us from the love of Christ? shall tribulation, or distress, or persecution, or famine, or nakedness, or peril, or sword?" (Romans 8:35), and then answers, "I am persuaded, that neither death, nor life, nor angels, nor principalities, nor powers, nor things present, nor things to come, nor height, nor depth, nor any other creature, shall be able to separate us from the love of God, which is in Christ Jesus our Lord" (Romans 8:38, 39).

And how can one in this age of multiple distractions maintain the single-minded sincerity that salvation requires?
Only as did Paul, by counting all else as subsidiary to the
cross. In spiritual matters, as in secular pursuits, success is
to a large degree determined by clarity of focus. *Attitude* de-
termines *altitude;* "we all grow in the direction of our rever-
ences." Many individuals capable of more noble achievements
have been stymied or diminished simply by lack of resolve.
Success in character building is not a matter of choice or
luck. It is first and most enduringly focusing upon the goal
of Christ-likeness. One must be set, in Isaiah's terminology,
"like a flint" (Isaiah 50:7) to hear and obey the voice of God.

And then the race begins! After instructing the runners to
their marks and warning them to "get set," the starter's gun is
fired, and the command is given: "Go!" This third and final
command is precisely what Paul has in mind when he writes,
"Forgetting those things which are behind, and reaching forth
unto those things which are before, I press toward the mark."
Paul does not leave the runners on their knees or tensely
poised, preparing to run. He describes himself, and us by inference, as now moving forward in earnest effort toward the
goal. And his "Go!" philosophy is exciting. It involves *"Forgetting those things which are behind."* It is a dangerous act for a
sprinter to look backward. Perhaps it can be risked in longer
races, but looking behind breaks the concentration, alters the
stride, affects the runner's rhythm—it is lethal to the
sprinter's cause.

Paul's reference to forgetting those things which are behind
is not an example of ingratitude on Paul's part. He was ever
grateful for God's mercies and people's kindnesses. He com-
ments on being thankful for the faith of his converts (see
Romans 1:8), for the witness of his converts (see 1 Thessalonians 1:2, 3, 9), for his gift of witness (see 1 Timothy 1:12), for
his associates in witness (see 2 Corinthians 8:16), for the grace
of Jesus (see 2 Corinthians 9:11), and for victory through
Jesus (see 2 Corinthians 2:14). No, what Paul means by "forgetting those things which are behind" is not to ignore past

benefits. What he means is that we must not be relaxed by past successes or cowed by past failures. Paul's words, "Forgetting those things which are behind," are a reminder that it is *today* that counts—this assignment, this job, this school year, and, in a fundamental sense, this day of my life with God.

The capacity to "close the books" on bygone events and eras is critical to present achievements. It is essential to intuit the transition points of life. We need to feel the shifting gears of time, to identify and demarcate new eras of opportunity, to realize change, to know where the track switches, when the rocket separates from the booster. We must understand and appreciate each period of life for its own peculiar challenges of growth and maturity.

Paul often demonstrated this sense of life's progressions. In this vein, he wrote to the Corinthians, "When I was a child, I spake as a child, I understood as a child, I thought as a child: but when I became a man, I put away childish things" (1 Corinthians 13:11). And he was in a like mood near the end of his life when he said to Timothy, "I have fought a good fight, I have finished my course, I have kept the faith: henceforth there is laid up for me a crown of righteousness which the Lord, the righteous judge, shall give me at that day" (2 Timothy 4:7-9).

But forgetting those things which are behind is not enough. Paul's action principle also includes *"Reaching to those things which are before."* Oliver Wendell Holmes said, "You can get run over in the right road if you just sit there." That is true on the highways of the land, it is true in our professional endeavors, and it is true in our spiritual journey, as well. The objectives are ahead. And the length of one's stride, the lean of the body, the action of the limbs—all mechanics of running perfected in training—must be utilized to the maximum to achieve the goal.

Those things which are before beckon us to do our best. They include our personal goals, our private hopes and ambitions, our family aims, our civic responsibilities, our church priorities, and, most importantly, those things before involve the salvation requirements of holiness, purity, godliness—elements of a Christ-like character. And our Lord is our best example here. His is the highest model.

Hebrews 12:2 states that He "for the joy that was set before him endured the cross, despising the shame." His way was hindered, His lot was bitter, His visage was marred more than that of any man—He trod the winepress alone. But because our salvation was before Him, He endured the temptations of the wilderness, the agonies of Gethsemane, and the pain of the cross. He looked beyond His agony to the joys before Him—and so must we.

The agony that Christ endured is reflected in Paul's amplification of what it means to "reach." His words are, "I press toward the mark." Moffatt's translation records him as saying, "[I am] straining to what lies before me." Straining is an all-out effort. It is no halfhearted, insipid, languid attempt at succeeding. It is a total try—a complete commitment, a hard-hitting do-or-die "full-court press," a never-say-never kind of determination to accomplish.

And straining begins before the race. First Corinthians 9:25 reads:

> Now every athlete who goes into training conducts himself temperately and restricts himself in all things. They do it to win a wreath that will soon wither, but we [do it to receive a crown of eternal blessedness] that cannot wither (Amplified Bible).

It is not easy to run for miles in the morning while others are asleep, to refuse desserts, to go to bed before the exciting programs come on TV. But Paul says that's the way to train for victory: "I buffet my body, handle it roughly, discipline it by hardships." I do push-ups, sit-ups, knee bends. I stretch my sinews and strengthen my muscles by running with weights around my ankles, and my temperate lifestyle and vigorous exercise prepare me for arduous, pressing effort during my performance on the field of endeavor.

Another passage that illuminates Paul's efforts in this

regard is Hebrews 12:1, where he states,

> Since we are surrounded by so great a cloud of witnesses . . . let us strip off and throw aside every encumbrance—unnecessary weight—and that sin which so readily . . . clings to and entangles us, and let us run with patient endurance and steady and active persistence the appointed course of the race that is set before us (Amplified Bible).

Now, Paul states, the race is on, and the weights are off. My body, primed by abstinence, and strengthened by exercise, responds with maximum strength. So it must be for us. Maximum mobility in our spiritual race requires us to jettison all extraneous weights, to cast aside not only sins but "shortcomings," to rid ourselves of what may not be "tests of fellowship" but are nevertheless inhibiting to spiritual progress, to rid ourselves of not just the conspicuous transgressions but also the little foxes that spoil the vine. Stripped down to the bare essentials, we can then run, straining to the mark which is before.

But know that it will never be easy. Satan will see to that. Life's goals are never reached in a single bound to success or by uninterrupted flights to shining diadems of accomplishment. We must press toward our mark. "Sanctification is the work of a lifetime," and we must strain through sunshine and rain, clear and cloudy days—sometimes over uneven terrain, sometimes through dark valleys, sometimes when the footing is slow and the road is winding and all uphill. But we must not quit. We must ever strive to work out our salvation with fear and trembling (see Philippians 2:12).

And what is the prize? It is a crown of life, the same described by Paul in 1 Corinthians 9:25 as a crown of eternal blessedness that cannot wither.

One of the most memorable experiences of my life occurred on a sunlit Sunday afternoon in Los Angeles when I was seventeen years of age. Upon recommendations from various other groups in the city, an organization of women gave awards to teenagers and young adults for accomplishments in various areas of community life. Trophies were passed out for achievements in track and field, academic pursuits, community services, musical performance, art, journalism, and religious endeavor. To my surprise and delight, I was chosen to be awarded in the last category.

What a day! The air was electric. Choirs, bands, banners, and a large crowd of people gathered at the old Memorial Field. Believe it or not, a throne had been erected in the general area of the pitcher's mound, and our names were called out over the loudspeaker. One by one we went up the stairs to the platform to be awarded. How proud I was of my trophy! How carefully I handled it and watched it and shined it and guarded it for several years.

But as time went by, my little trophy lost its luster literally and psychologically. By the time I finished college, it was little more than a figure on the whatnot shelf in the family room, and when I married, it was relegated to the study, and by the time our children arrived, it became a curiosity piece, tarnished by time and dropped, broken, and desecrated by my own flesh and blood. Oh, I still have it. But I scarcely look at it and never (except in a situation such as this) even mention it. When I do, it is only to emphasize the fragility of earthly awards, as compared to the quality of everlasting life.

Since for us the ultimate goal is Christ-likeness and the final prize life everlasting, we must be willing to make whatever sacrifices necessary for victory and to run faithfully the course before us. No other commitment is worthy of such bestowals. No other bestowals can claim such dedication.

We must say with the intrepid apostle, "Brethren, I count not myself to have apprehended: but this one thing I do, forgetting those things which are behind, and reaching forth unto those things which are before, I press toward the mark for the prize of the high calling of God in Jesus Christ."

While God looks to our lives for growth in holiness, He does not look to our lives for final acceptability. Recognizing our human condition—the ongoing, ever-present struggle that He knows we have with our unholy flesh—He has provided final and full acceptance through Christ.

Chapter 13

The Body and the I Myself

"For I delight in the law of God after the inward man: but I see another law in my members, warring against the law of my mind, and bringing me into captivity to the law of sin which is in my members. . . . So then with the mind I myself serve the law of God; but with the flesh the law of sin" (Romans 7:22-25).

One of the traits of Greek philosophy that carried over into early Christian thought was the use of the rhetorical device known as "logical dualism." This characteristic, very common to ancient literary endeavors, was the tendency to portray reality in terms of polarized antagonists. Paul's theology is laced with such tensions. This is seen in his contrasts of (1) sin versus righteousness, (2) the flesh versus the Spirit, (3) faith versus sight, (4) the "already" versus the "not yet," (5) our "sinful once" versus our "converted now," (6) the old man versus the new man, and (7) the wishes of the sinful "outer" man versus the earnest strivings of the more obedient "inner" man. It is the latter polarity that he uses in Romans 7. Here, the outer man is the physical body where originate and triumph the urges of the flesh; the inner man is the *nous*—the intellectual creature inside the *soma*, or the corporeal being.

In Paul's thought, these two selves, the visible body and the invisible man, are ever at odds. They differ in orientation and desire, and consistent with the dualistic thinking of Paul's day, are locked in unending conflict. Thus, in describing his own spiritual struggle, he wrote: "I delight in the law of God after the inward man: but I see another law in my members, warring against the law of my mind. . . . So then with the mind [the inner man] I myself serve the law of God; but with the flesh [the outer man] the law of sin" (Romans 7:22-25).

Now, it is debatable whether or not the apostle really believed that each of us is a dual personality. He would, of course, be no less a man of God if he did. Even the prophets are limited by the sociohistorical understandings of their times. Our concern, however, is not for the sophistication of Paul's psychology or the accuracy of his physiology—nor even the literalness of his theology. What we really must understand is (a) the complexity of his spiritual dilemma and (b) his method of resolving this highly conflictual relationship. Just how severe was the cleavage between the two selves that polarized his being? And how did Paul resolve this troublesome dilemma?

First we must look at the nature of the conflict, or the depth of the frustration that he experienced. Verse 23 states the case succinctly: "I see another law in my members, warring against the law of my mind." It is not a discussion, not a debate, nor even a heated argument, but a real, live war that rages between the body of his sensual flesh and the conscience of his rational self.

A view of the two words that the New Testament utilizes to designate warfare help clarify the point. The Greek word used by Jesus in Matthew 24:6 when He states, "Ye shall hear of wars and rumours of wars," and by John in Revelation 12:7, "There was war in heaven," is *polimos*. However, when Paul urges his young friend Timothy to fight a good fight of faith (see 1 Timothy 1:18), and when Peter in 1 Peter 2:11 speaks of fleshly lusts as *war* in the body, the word they use is *strateuo*.

The difference is that, with one notable exception (see James 4:2), *polimos* is a noun, a subject or event about which we learn or which is witnessed. *Strateuo,* on the other hand, is used as a verb. It is the word that is employed in 2 Corinthians 10:3 and 2 Timothy 2:4 and James 4:1, where the writer sees himself or another in live combat against an enemy. Paul gives this thought its clearest meaning in Romans 7:23, where he characterizes the warfare that he is undergoing as anti-*strateuo.* *Strateuo* is not strong enough. The prefix *anti* here adds a sense of radical hostility between the outer and inner man. This is not simply a war. It is the bitterest of wars, a civil war, the crazed hatred of forces once united, brothers estranged by sin, now locked in mortal conflict.

The negative effect of the outer man's molestations on the inner man's tranquility is seen in three graphic figures. Verse 14 of Romans 7 contains the first of these analogies. His words are: "We know that the law is spiritual: but I am carnal, sold under sin." Here Paul likens himself to a *slave,* one whose inner man (the *I myself*) protests its servitude but who is nevertheless forever indentured to the realities of his nature.

The language of his second analogy is given in verse 20: "If I do that I would not, it is no more I that do it, but sin that dwelleth in me." This second figure is that of a virus—a *contagion*—it is not really the *I myself* whom Paul sees as responsible. Since the inner man sins despite wanting to do otherwise, the fault must be in some other force (the inherited, inescapable affliction of evil propensity). And that for Paul seems an incurable disease.

The third figure that Paul expands upon in this dilemma is presented in verse 23: "I see another law in my members, warring against the law of my mind, and bringing me into captivity." Here is Paul the *prisoner.* First, he is a slave sold under sin. Second, he is victim of an incurable contagion. Now, handcuffed by sin, he typifies his situation as that of the lawbreaker. Trapped, overcome, and incarcerated, he is not just a slave or one afflicted with a disease. He is handcuffed by sin, hostage to powers that refuse to negotiate his freedom.

Some thoughtful theologians imply that Paul is not speaking about himself in this passage. It is impossible, they reason, for him to be such a sinner and at the same time an acceptable, productive apostle. But when we count the personal references throughout the chapter, we note that Paul uses the first-person nominative *I* thirty-three times, the objective *me* twelve times, *we* six times, *my* four times, *our* two times, and *myself* once. There are a total of fifty-six usages of personal pronouns in these few versus.

Paul was used to contribute thirteen books of the Sacred Canon, and for years traveled throughout the civilized world, baptizing and building up God's work. How could this apostle be in such dire straits? How could he possibly say that one part of him was willing to serve God but that the other still lusted after base satisfactions? The following statement helps us understand:

> All may now obtain holy hearts, but it is not correct to claim in this life to have holy flesh. The apostle Paul declares, "I know that in me (that is, in my flesh,) dwelleth no good thing" (Rom. 7:18). To those who have tried so hard to obtain by faith so-called holy flesh, I would say, You cannot obtain it. Not a soul of you has holy flesh now. . . . It is an impossibility (*Selected Messages*, bk. 2, p. 32).

Ever wonder why, even after conversion, we still struggle with inherited and cultivated tendencies to evil? The answer is that each of us is afflicted with the unshakable burden of sinful flesh, a dynamo of never-ending impulses to pride and lustful aggrandizement. Paul's anthropology is correct. It is a fundamental fact of the human condition that sinful flesh is retained even after conversion. The seeds of carnal desire remain in even the most advanced Christian states. Thus, the necessity to "die daily" and our never-ceasing efforts to overcome.

And that brings us to a most critical question. How does the apostle resolve his dilemma? Obviously, he is not happy with the reality of his condition. He wants to kick his habits once and for all. He wants to "get the monkey off his back"—to stop eating so much, to control his temper, to cease his judgmentalism; he wants to cease foolish thinking, to stop his craving for mindless music and trashy literature, his use of foul language, his desire for revenge, his love of pleasure, his quest for material things, his combativeness, his wish to be number one, and his wasting of time.

And he desires victory not only over sins of commission but those of omission as well. He wishes to throw away the weights that so easily beset, to remove the asterisks that keep him from being exactly like his Lord. Thus, he cries out in despair, "O wretched man that I am! who shall deliver me from the body of this death?" (Romans 7:24). Is there no emancipation possible? Is there no healing for his disease? No balm in Gilead? Who will free him from his bondage? Then he reflects upon the efficacy of the blood of Christ and exclaims joyfully: "I thank God through Jesus Christ" (verse 25).

I'm glad that the apostle didn't leave us groveling on the wrestling mat of sin, forever grappling with the debilitating consequences of our carnality. This wretched, pitiable, helpless creature does have hope! There is a balm in Gilead. There is a way out, and that is through Jesus Christ.

How does Christ accomplish our deliverance? Our first step toward resolution is the conversion of the inner man. We have been very critical of the outer man, but let's not forget that the inner man is not too swift either. It is the inner man, the "I myself," of which David speaks when he confesses of being "born in sin and shapen in iniquity." To his eternal credit, however, the inner man is amenable to conversion. God can talk to the inner man. The inner man can be born again. Before he is converted, the inner man is in perfect accord with the outer man. They travel the same path, talk the same language—they are partners in crime. It is when conversion takes place that the struggle begins, and the very reality of the struggle is a sign of progress, a sure token that the outer man no longer rules uncontested and unrestrained, that Christ now has residence with the inner man, and that the battle for eternal life has begun.

The second element of resolution is the gradual weakening of the outer man's power by one of the oldest combat techniques known to humanity—starvation! Buttressed by the Word of God, the inner man now engages in the process of refusal—refusing to eat, read, speak, think, or do the dictates of the outer self. There will be times when we fail, times when we falter, and when, faithless and forgetful, we yield to the dictates of sin. But the predominant pattern resulting from the infusion of Christ's power is obedience to God's will and denial of the flesh. The flesh denied is the flesh diminished. No longer fed the slime and slop that it needs for strength, the outer man becomes inoperative. And while the outer man is lessened by denial, the inner man grows strong by feeding upon "whatsoever things are true, whatsoever things are honest, whatsoever things are just, whatsoever things are pure, whatsoever things are lovely, whatsoever things are of good report" (Philippians 4:8). The impoverished outer man—alive but subdued—no longer controls us. Now it is not the body, but the "I myself" who rules through the power of Christ.

A third and final aspect of the process is Christ's act of covering us with His robe of righteousness. It is not enough that the inner man is converted. Unholy flesh is a contamination unworthy of God's presence. Struggling, fighting, erring, it disqualifies us for membership among the undefiled of heaven. We cannot qualify for approbation "doing what we would not and not doing what we should." Our marks of Cain distinguish us as strivers but still sinners, believers but still beleaguered. This is why Christ's robe is mandated. We are destined to carry our troublesome, unholy flesh until we die, and we do not qualify for heaven after we expire. Seeing our dilemma, Christ substitutes His robe of righteousness for our rags of humanity, and God accepts this replacement, counting us as righteous—worthy of approval.

But even then the struggle continues. We are converted, we are covered, we are accepted, but God does not take away our unholy flesh. Rather, He equips us for overcoming it, and He makes up for our deficiencies through the process of substitution.

And how did it all end for the apostle? Well, finally, when he came to die he looked back at his Christian journey and wrote: "I have fought a good fight, I have finished my course, I have kept the faith: henceforth there is laid up for me a crown of righteousness." Notice this is not a claim of absolute perfection, but a confession of a good try and a fervent belief in reward and renewal of body and soul at the coming of the Lord.

Did I say that the outer man is not amenable to change? That is true now, but he will be changed at the coming of Christ. First Corinthians 15:51, 52 promises that we shall all be changed at the twinkling of an eye. We can forgive Paul for evidently accepting the inner man/outer man construct as a reality. It is only our distance from Greek philosophy that allows us to use this analogy without seeing it as factual. But even so, when we confess that "we have no holy flesh," we are admitting that our minds are permanently damaged by sin. Our flesh is not operated by a unit outside ourselves. The indictment of the flesh is, in reality, an indictment of the mind, the apparatus that controls it.

But we can have "holy hearts," that is, wills that are completely yielded to Christ. A sanctified will results from Christ's occupying the soul's temple and thus subduing of the carnal nature. It is the core element of our sanctification and our only hope for overcoming. But when, at His coming, Christ transposes our now-holy wills into uncorrupted (holy) flesh—the flesh of Adam before he sinned—the warfare will be over. The dilemma solved, our appetites and wills will then be reunited, no longer antagonists, but partners again in the service of the creature.

My favorite illustration for the restoration that God will provide via translation and/or resurrection is that of a caterpillar that crossed over a busy highway. The caterpillar, so the story goes, wanted to cross the wide road and stuck its head out from among the leaves and began the slow process of inching its way across the pavement. Heavy vibrations told it that traffic rumbled down the road, so the hapless creature recoiled and pulled itself back under a muddy leaf, despairing and discouraged. Then, when it thought the way was clear, it started across the highway again. But it hadn't gone very far when once more it felt the tremors of danger and retreated to its place of safety.

The process continued time and again. Finally the pitiful creature crawled under some muddy leaves and simply gave up the struggle. And when it did, nature mercifully wrapped a cocoon about it to protect it from the elements. Soon the summer sun had waned, the autumn winds had blown, and the snows fell upon the creature now buried securely in its covering. There it stayed for weeks and months until another cycle of time arrived. The spring sun melted the snow, and the spring winds blew away the leaves, revealing a little cocoon now exposed to the piercing rays of the April sun. Those rays beat upon that cocoon until it dried, cracked, and opened. When it had unfolded sufficiently, out came not the ugly caterpillar it had been, but a beautiful, multicolored butterfly with scintillating wings. And, leaving its burial ground in the mud, the transformed beauty flitted across the highway it could not traverse and on to the fields beyond.

I see another drama today. I see a whole human race bound up and restricted by sin. I see us struggling, striving for perfection. I see us wrestling with ourselves, arguing with ourselves, fighting with ourselves. I see our spiritual disability and our need for further growth and overcoming. I see our dissatisfaction with our present state. The ultimate seems always beyond our grasp. And finally, we lie down in death, hounded to the end by the braying of the flesh, destined to bear the body of death, and we finally pay the penalty of death.

But God's promise is that one day the trumpet will sound and the Son of Righteousness will speak words that shall pierce the cocoons of our graves. What will emerge will not be the sin-scarred creatures of this mortal world, but the glorious bodies of the redeemed now freed from the curse, no longer under the tensions of the body and the "I myself," but under the divine rule of perfection and perpetual harmony of body and soul.